SEEDS

Sasha Vukelja, M.D.

KACHA HOUSE

© 2009 by Svetislava J. Vukelja

Seeds: A Memoir

Published in the United States of America

KACHA HOUSE

978-0-578-02313-7 *(paperback)*
978-0-578-02314-4 *(hardcover)*

Produced with the assistance of
Fluency Organization, Inc. in Tyler, Texas.
Book design by Diane Kronmeyer. Cover design by Richard Danne.

Original cover artwork by Katarina Maksimovich. "Mojstrana" oil on canvas.

Visit us online at www.seedsthebook.com

To Mama

Katarina Maksimovich

ACKNOWLEDGMENTS

Where my life is at this point is a product of the giving and sharing of all the people and patients I have met, and many more will be there in the future.

I am grateful to all of them—it would be a very long list of names. They know who they are.

So to all of you, thank you. For planting, watering and nurturing all the seeds in my life. May this book help you see the seeds God is planting in your lives.

CONTENTS

I am of the opinion that my life belongs to the whole community, and as long as I live it is my privilege to do for it whatever I can. I want to be thoroughly used up when I die, for the harder I work the more I live. I rejoice in life for its own sake. Life is no "brief candle" for me. It is a sort of splendid torch which I have got hold of for the moment, and I want to make it burn as brightly as possible before handing it on to future generations.

George Bernard Shaw

END OF THE BEGINNING

Washington, DC, 1985

I TASTED THE SALTY TEARS THAT WERE RUNNING DOWN MY face and bathing the corners of my lips. Everything around me seemed blurred, and my overwhelming grief muffled the roar of the jet engines outside the tiny window. I closed my swollen eyes and leaned back in the large, first class seat. I had never flown first class before. A kind airline attendant appeared, softly asking if I wanted something to drink. I just needed to be alone with my thoughts for a while, so I managed a weak smile and told her no.

At that moment, the biggest fear I had was that I would go insane. I was terrified I would arrive back home and start walking down the street—without recognizing anyone and without knowing who I was. I felt so lost and prayed for help to continue thinking clearly. My mother had been all the family I had in America; now I had no one. Of all the places I could be when she died, I was thousands of miles away, visiting my friends in Alaska.

After receiving news of my mother's sudden death, I flew back home to Washington, DC, where my mother and I lived. I remember my desperation for answers regarding her death. *How long did it take?* I wondered. *How much did she suffer?* As I am an oncologist, family members had often asked me similar questions about their loved ones who had died from cancer. Now I fully recognized how deep the need to know can go. I longed for someone to tell me my mother did not suffer. That she did not gasp for air, all alone. When I received the emergency call from her physician, he had said, simply, "It was a natural death."

But there was nothing natural about her death. It was anything but natural for my mother to die at age 62, when I was fighting every day to help people much older and sicker than her to go on living. I wanted to see her body. Until I did, I could not believe Mama was gone.

As a doctor, I am familiar with death, but I don't claim to understand it. There is more to living than what modern medical equipment can monitor. There is an indefinable spark, what some call a person's soul or spirit. When someone dies, that spark is snuffed out like a smoldering candle wick. I've witnessed it many times. Suddenly that mass of flesh on the bed no longer represents a person at all. They're gone. After a patient dies, another patient moves into the same hospital room, oblivious to what transpired there just hours before. Someone's life spark disappeared into the mysterious, crisp white folds of the sheets in that same bed, in that same room. And now they have gone.

My flight from Alaska connected to another flight, and I had to change planes. My face was so swollen and my eyelids so puffy that I could hardly keep them open as I exited the plane. My nose was running, my lips were red and it felt as if my whole body was experiencing an allergic reaction to the intense pain I felt in my heart. I was trying not to cry, walking slowly through the airport to the next gate. What I needed at that moment was to absorb the warmth and hug from another human being. I longed for someone to caress my hair, hold me and tell me everything was going to be okay. But the airport was so cold. Everyone and everything was rushing by me, unfeeling and uncaring.

I'd grown to dislike airports because they represented goodbyes, separation and change. I hated to move. From the time I was a young girl in Yugoslavia, my mother and I were constantly relocating. We never stayed in one city or village for more than several months at a time until I was in college.

I was born Svetislava Vukelja in 1951 in Ljubljana, the capital of Slovenia, one of the six republics in Yugoslavia. My mother had just been released from exile as a political prisoner, and she was pregnant with me. She expected a difficult delivery, and I was, in fact, a breech baby—just the kind of case that Dr. Laurich, my mother's obstetrician in Ljubljana, was famous for handling.

Mama was told that Dr. Laurich's brother had delivered two sons for the Italian movie star, Sophia Loren. My mother reasoned that if his brother could do such a fine job for Ms. Loren, Dr. Laurich was capable of delivering me. At my birth, there were no presents or cards from my grandmother or my aunt (on my mother's side). In fact, I recall receiving only one gift from them in my entire childhood—a burgundy turtleneck sweater with matching, opaque burgundy pantyhose. To me, the outfit looked as though I was seeping blood from head to toe. I had cropped hair and only wore boys' pants at the time, so the pantyhose were wasted on me.

I always felt my grandmother tried to hide my mother and me and erase our very existence. In fact, some of my grandmother's friends in Belgrade, where she lived, never even knew she had two daughters. However, our presence was no secret to the Communists. They tracked our every movement.

SEEDS

From the time I was a young child, we were moving every three to six months to keep my mother's past as a political refugee from catching up with her.

My schooling was sporadic. Just when I settled into one school, I would have to start over in a new place. I don't remember the names of any of my grade school teachers—there were so many. The other kids sensed my insecurity, and I became a magnet for their teasing. They struck me and said all kinds of mean things to me, calling my mother and me names. I never had a best friend or even a playmate. My mother was my only friend and companion. In all our travels, we carried very little with us from place to place and never once dared to call somewhere "home."

If I did meet friends, it was safer to think of them as acquaintances, because I never knew when I would have to leave, never to see their faces again. I never knew other children well enough to confide any of my secrets, nor to share theirs. Instead, my childhood is a tumbleweed of jumbled memories, blowing aimlessly from place to place. The wind would blow and the seeds would scatter once again, never having a chance to establish roots. It would be eleven years of this transient existence in Yugoslavia before Mama and I could legally immigrate to Austria.

Mama alone knew the world I'd grown up in—at that time in my life, she *was* my world. Her death marked the end of my beginning. I had no idea where to go from there—I only knew I would have to do so alone.

* * *

AFTER I MADE the connecting flight that would take me home to Washington, DC, the time passed very slowly. Exhausted

4

and unable to cry anymore, I could only stare into the distance. My mother's friends, Dianka and her husband John, were waiting for me at the gate when I arrived. Although they tried to comfort me, I still felt paralyzed with grief. Unfortunately, it was too late to go to the funeral home that night. I would have to wait until the next day. "I have to see her," I kept telling myself. "I just want to see her."

The next day we went to the funeral home and a Czechoslovakian woman greeted us. I didn't recognize her at first when she came into the well-decorated parlor where we were waiting, but she was one of my mother's neighbors, and happened to work there. She said something about being sorry about my mother, and I nodded.

My mother and this lady had met one day at the mailbox. Mama had eaten dinner with her and her husband on occasion, and they often told her funny stories about life in a funeral home. One time an immigrant family had asked the funeral home if they could keep their relative's body another week while they waited on the rest of the family to arrive from overseas. This was against the funeral home's policy, but my mother's Czech friend and her husband offered to store the body in their living room instead. In place of the coffee table, they rearranged the couch and television to make room for the casket. When Mama told me the story, we laughed about how much money they must have made that week.

This former neighbor would be the one to make up my mother's face. Since she had known my mother personally, I felt confident that she would know what Mama looked like and would remember that she did not wear makeup. After talking with me for a minute, she directed me to a room where I had to sign papers—so many papers. Then I ordered cards and thank-you notes and picked out a coffin. To add to the stress, my savings were tied up in the S&L crisis going on at that time, and I could not access the money in my account. The thought haunted me that although I was a doctor, I could not pay to bury my own mother. Desperate, I quietly went to several friends to borrow money to cover the funeral expenses.

In this little room, dozens of coffins lined the walls ranging in price from $600 to $5000 each. There was a mahogany coffin with red velvet. I knew how much my mother loved mahogany. There were also metal coffins that fit inside steel cases—something the funeral home director described as having "double protection."

"Nothing will be able to go in here," he said assuredly, as he tapped the side of the cold, gray casing.

I'd had nightmares after seeing one too many horror movies with bugs and worms crawling over decomposing bodies. I couldn't bear that happening to my mother, so the information about double protection was not lost on me. I wanted the most secure coffin available.

In the middle of this sterile decision-making, I soon realized that the funeral home was just a business focused on capitalizing on other people's pain—and even guilt—in order to sell as much as they could. I felt they were exploiting my loss: everything had a price tag.

When I picked out the less expensive, metal coffin with "double protection" instead of the more expensive mahogany one, I saw the Czech lady shoot me a guilt-provoking stare. *How could I deny the best for my mother—me, the wealthy doctor?*

Fortunately, Dianka, who was also from Yugoslavia, was more pragmatic and quickly eased the burden. "It really does not matter, Sasha," she said. "It doesn't make a difference what you are buried in…once you're dead, you're dead."

They told us to come back the next day, when my mother would be "ready for viewing." I was emotionally drained from dealing with the business of death.

The weather was warm in DC, but I was still wearing the wool socks, sweater and khaki pants that I had packed for my Alaska trip. That evening, Dianka and I shared two glasses of Manischewitz wine before I went to sleep on the sofa in their living room. They tried to cook for me, but I had no appetite.

* * *

THE FUNERAL was very simple. People came from Children's Hospital in DC, where I had previously worked as a nurse, along with my peers and colleagues from Walter Reed Army Medical Center where I was now a doctor. I wore a black blouse with lace and a gray wool skirt that hung from my frame because of all the weight I had lost that week.

There were other acquaintances of my mother's at the funeral that I did not know, including people from the senior center where my mother had started going. Of course, there were people there we both knew—most of whom Mama had recently stopped talking to because she blamed them for influencing me to move out of the apartment we shared and be more independent. I knew Dianka and her husband were some of those people.

In fact, we had been at Dianka's house for Easter dinner last spring when Mama and I had a major disagreement. I can't even remember what it was about, but that evening, I left home and I never came back. Now it was barely autumn and my mother was dead. I remembered her words, "The sadness of your leaving home will kill me." I wondered now if her words were somehow prophetic.

I did not cry at all the day of the funeral; I felt emotionally empty. When it was over, I somehow gathered the strength to thank everyone for coming. The burial on a grassy hill, under a large oak tree, was very quiet. Most of the people had to return to work at the hospital. I had to go back to work the next week, after I cleaned out my mother's apartment.

My father had died in Yugoslavia many years before, when I was a young adult, just months before my mother and I immigrated to America. I felt that my mother had died too soon, just like my father. He never knew how life changed for us in America. He never heard that I went to college, that I finished medical school or that I became a doctor. My father saw my life, but only as one sees a handful of seeds: nameless, faceless potential that may or may not amount to much. Mama was the one who saw the tiny seeds take root and the seedlings start to grow. But she died before the blooms could fully open and unfold to the sun's warmth. Maybe she always knew that day would come, but it did not happen in time for me to show her or to prove to her I could do it. To let her touch the fragile petals with her fingertips.

* * *

AFTER THE FUNERAL, I turned my attention to my mother's apartment. We had only been in America for thirteen years, but it was long enough for my mother to fill her home with memories from our life both in America and Yugoslavia.

My mother started collecting paintings when we lived in Belgium. She always said that she adopted all the unknown painters—mostly Dutch—and some of the pieces were very good. However, the bulk of canvasses scattered throughout the small rooms were ones she had painted herself: nearly eight hundred in all, of every shape and size.

I was sitting alone on her apartment floor, feeling strangely comforted by the piles of opened, weathered family albums surrounding me, when I suddenly remembered the brown canvas bag. I jumped up, opened a hall closet and found it exactly where I expected it to be. My mother never let this bag out of her sight. Inside, a collection of worn, folded documents and dog-eared photographs told a story. Her story. And that is important because in order to understand my story, another story must first be understood. One that begins a world away with a young woman named Katarina Maksimovich—my mother.

SEEDS

CHAPTER TWO

HER SISTER'S
SHADOW

"**M**IA! MIA CARA!" HE CRIED AS HE MADE HIS WAY over to Katarina. *My dear, my dear.*

He was a striking Italian man in uniform with an easy smile and irrepressibly charming accent. It was the spring of 1941 and my mother, Katarina Maksimovich, was eighteen years old. Her mother, Persida Stanich Maksimovich (known as "Sida"), had sent Katarina into the city to check on the apartment they shared in Belgrade, the capital of what was then Yugoslavia. The Germans had just bombed the city, as retribution for Yugoslavia essentially "switching sides" and joining the Allies. Yugoslavia's act of defiance had incensed Hitler and resulted in immediate orders for the German Luftwaffe to bomb Belgrade for several days, beginning on Palm Sunday. Most citizens, including my family, had evacuated the city to nearby villages until the final wave of bombing was over.

Now Katarina stared at the bold, Italian stranger. Startled by his bravado, she stood outside the family apartment building, puzzling over the man who was making his way towards her. He took her hand in his and kissed it gently.

"Siete molto bella, Signorita." *You are very beautiful, Miss.*

Katarina let a small smile escape her lips. She spoke fairly good Italian herself, and it was clear that this man was flirting with her. The soldier's buddies hovered nearby, laughing like schoolboys, but he just ignored their taunts. He looked at Katarina as no man had ever looked at her in her life.

For the first time, she felt that a man *saw* her.

Katarina had grown up in the shadow of her younger sister, Kosana, who was her mother's favorite. Her mother Sida criticized Katarina constantly, drawing unfavorable comparisons between the two sisters. "Koka," as the younger sister was called, was a dark-eyed girl of raven beauty. In this she resembled her mother, whose wisps of coal black hair fluttered against alluring dark eyes and milky white skin. People often mistook Sida and Koka for sisters. This no doubt pleased my grandmother immensely.

In fact, Sida never let the girls call her "Mama" in public. She was a very proud and vain woman. "Kacha," as Katarina was called, looked more like her father, who had died when she was a little girl. Her hair wound together in curls, and her hazel eyes blended into her rather plain, olive-toned face. She could pass for a Jew, with her prominent nose. In fact, during the war she was often stopped on the street and interrogated by officials who wanted to know why she wasn't wearing the yellow star patch on her clothing, as was required for all Jews.

"No one is ever going to marry you, Kacha," Sida would often say to her, shaking her head in obvious disappointment. When Kacha looked in the mirror at night before retiring to bed, she must have wondered sometimes if what her mother said was, in fact, true.

So when Kacha saw that she alone was the object of this handsome soldier's desire, she reveled in his attention. As if they had known each other years instead of hours, they spent the afternoon talking and laughing together.

His name was Nino. Nino Cardarullo.

She was glad for the Italian lessons she'd taken in school, since she could understand most of what he was saying and converse with him as well. At some point in the day, the pair exchanged an outrageous thought: they must marry. That day. I imagine it was a desperate move on my mother's part. Her country was at war, and this might be her only chance to marry.

A kind young priest agreed to marry the couple in a Catholic church that afternoon. My mother stayed in Belgrade three more days, still presumably checking on the apartment, so she could be with her new love.

And then, as quickly as he had appeared on the street corner, Nino was gone.

He rejoined his unit as they made their way to the frontlines of the war. My grandmother and Koka soon joined Kacha back at the apartment and began resettling their things. Kacha never breathed a word to them about her secret. One day they heard a loud knock at the front door. Sida opened it to find two Italian soldiers standing in her doorway.

"Is Signora Cardarullo here, please?" one of the men inquired. Thinking they must be looking for another woman, Sida informed them that there was no Signora in their household.

"Only Signoritas, gentlemen. You have the wrong apartment." She smiled politely and began to shut the door in their faces.

Just then, one of the men raised his hand against the doorway and looked over Sida's shoulder. "Ah, there she is! Signora Cardarullo." Kacha had been peeking around the corner of the hallway, listening to their conversation. She stood frozen in place as her eyes met Sida's angry glare.

"Katarina, what have you done now?" Sida asked, calling

her by her first name, as she did whenever Kacha was in trouble. My mother slowly made her way to her room and showed my grandmother the wedding license she had carefully hidden under her clothes. The two soldiers, now sitting in the kitchen, had been witnesses at the wedding. They brought news of Nino's whereabouts, and had been searching the city the entire morning trying to find his wife.

Nino was in the hospital. Three days after their whirlwind wedding, he had been marching with his unit and stepped on a land mine. Both of his legs had been amputated.

If Kacha expected to garner any sympathy from her mother over this tragedy, she was disappointed. Sida's terse advice to her was, "You made your bed, now you must sleep in it." My grandmother thought her oldest daughter had been particularly foolish on several counts. Marrying a perfect stranger—an Italian—and an enlisted man, at that. Now he was a cripple with no legs, no job and no money. Still, Sida was quick to insist that Kacha visit Nino in the hospital immediately to take care of him.

Kacha left to visit him, but not out of duty. She loved him. But what was there to say? They were strangers to each other now. The course of their lives had brought them together in a warm wave of passion, but now the waters had grown still and cool. Life had so suddenly changed forever.

Kacha visited Nino faithfully in the hospital for the next several days but arrived one morning to find his bed empty. His unit had been assigned to another part of the country, and Nino had been moved along with them.

My mother never saw her Italian husband again.

Over the next few months, she tried locating him through several appeals to the Red Cross, but to no avail. She was Greek

Orthodox, unaware of the Catholic Church's rules prohibiting divorce. Marrying Nino in a Catholic ceremony rendered her later attempts to annul the marriage useless. Her letters to the Vatican went unanswered. She didn't know whether her husband was alive, missing or dead, but she could not get divorced.

* * *

AFTER THE WAR was over, the political climate in Yugoslavia began to change. Josip Broz Tito led the country into a distinctive brand of communism that became known as Titoism. Although independent of the formal Communist party of Russia, it carried the same repressive flavor. The new regime snuffed out any flicker of perceived reluctance to join the party ranks. In a country that was becoming less and less free in terms of personal expression, Kacha grew more and more outspoken. Despite the risks, she could not keep from sharing her political viewpoints with anyone who would listen.

If Kacha was outspoken, another young Yugoslav named Ivan was even more so. He was often cited for a variety of "crimes" against the regime, though he never led a rebellion or subverted the government outright. His sharp mind and quick wit were the weapons that threatened the political beliefs of the Communists, so they tried to silence him. Every day, Ivan made his way down the city streets to a local newsstand, where he picked up the paper, quickly scanned the front page and threw the rest into the nearby trash bin.

The newspaper seller was curious about his actions and finally said one day, "You have been my customer for years. You buy the paper and look over the front page only to throw it all away. What are you looking for?"

15

Ivan coolly replied, "I'm looking for obituaries."

"Obituaries?" the man scoffed, raising one thick, dark eyebrow as he straightened a stack of his papers. "They're listed at the end of the paper, not the front."

"The man whose obituary I'm looking for is going to be on the front page," Ivan said with a wry smile. He patted the news carrier on the shoulder and briskly walked away.

Cracking a joke like this on a street corner was no small matter. People could report a person for something like that, and they did. Neighbors would disappear for six months at a time and then suddenly reappear as if nothing happened—if they came back at all. Despite the danger, Ivan's brilliant mind and determination kept him from being content to follow the crowd or go along with the mainstream.

Like Kacha, Ivan was strongly and willfully independent—an intellectual. They had both earned doctorates in Economics and were vocal in their views against the ruling party. The government responded quickly and mercilessly to any perceived threat, squelching dissenting opinions by either execution or exile. Of course, they could not kill everyone, so they often exiled the intellectuals to keep them from influencing other people with their ideas.

After several stints in prison, Ivan was eventually exiled to the small village of Kupres as punishment for his strong opinions. Later Kacha, then in her mid-twenties, was exiled to Kupres as well.

Isolating these young revolutionaries, keeping them from the stimulus of shared ideas and any opportunity to interact with other like-minded individuals was in some ways a fate worse than death. They had no freedom to express themselves, no freedom to talk with others and, worst of all, no audience.

It was in these lonely circumstances that Mama and my father, Ivan Vukelja, met.

*   *   *

MY FATHER HAD been in prison several times before he met my mother in Kupres. My mother also went to prison three times, serving one-year sentences each time. She always believed that they would have put her away for longer periods, but since the prosecutor was the brother of a friend, she was shown some leniency. During her imprisonment, they let her out into the sunlight once a day, and she fondly remembered once being allowed a special meal of eggs.

On several occasions, Kacha attempted to escape Yugoslavia. Once she tried to get through Bulgaria—the closest border visible from the city limits. However, at each attempt, they caught her and returned her to prison. This record of her escape attempts would haunt my mother long after I was born, when we were more than desperate to get out.

Mama used to tell me that my father had deep-set blue eyes so beautiful that no one could resist him, including herself. When Mama met my father, he had been separated from his first wife, Emitsa, for some time. He rarely saw his wife because he was in and out of prison so often. And, like my mother and Nino, the Catholic Church prohibited them from getting legally divorced.

When my mother arrived in Kupres, Ivan instantly fell in love with her—but their time together in exile proved to be short-lived, not even two years. When my mother was six months pregnant with me, my father was sent away to prison, where he would remain for the next nine years. Prior to leaving, however, he did something very valuable for my mother and me. He filed legal documents to claim me as his child, which is why I bear his last name. It was very important to my mother that I not be born a bastard child—that my father would declare me as his own.

He was Croatian and my mother was a Serb, although not purely so because she was originally from Montenegro. Croatians always felt they were slightly superior to the Serbs, so I was always especially quick to point out my father's heritage and introduce myself by my father's lineage. "I'm Croatian, but my mother is Serb," I would say, although as a child I did not fully understand the significance of this distinction.

I was about nine years old when I met my father for the first time, following his release from prison. I think my mother was proud that he came to see us before returning to Emitsa and his family.

Not knowing what I might like, he brought me three oranges and two children's books as a small gift. The details from that meeting are still so clear in my mind. Every smell, every sight, every word from that day seem weighted with significance in my memory. My father was wearing a thick wool sweater, with brown deer and two snowflakes crocheted on the front. I remember holding the oranges to my nose and breathing in their citrus smell. A single photograph, his sweater and these small gifts are my only remaining memories of my father.

I never saw him again after that day. He left that same afternoon to return to his first wife and family. My mother always said that spending nearly a decade in prison had drastically changed him. In prison, they had tortured him mercilessly, and my mother did not hesitate to explain the abuse to me in some detail.

We'd heard stories about the government skinning people alive and rolling their bodies in salt, freezing men's genitals or spearing babies on bayonets like kebabs. The mental images were horrible—and yet they were the harsh reality of the times. Somehow, we accepted it.

After being gone nine long years, my father told my mother that she "deserved better" than the man he had become. I thought, at the time, that his reasoning was providing him with a cowardly way out of the relationship.

Over the next few years, as my mother and I were forced to move from place to place like nomads, I blamed him for our situation. I felt that if my father had stayed with us our lives would be easier and we would have more stability. I don't know if that's true or not, but my childhood feelings lingered. I never really liked my father.

Despite my ambivalence and our estrangement, I convinced myself that I could still go live with him one day if I wished. When I was a teen, and Mama and I would disagree, I would threaten to leave her and go live with my father, although I would never have followed through. I didn't want to be with him, and I could not say for certain that he would have *wanted* me living with him. Outside of my memory from that day as a nine-year-old and the one picture I had of him as a young man in his uniform, I had little idea what he looked like.

My mother also toyed with the idea of sending me to my father. She even brought it up on a number of occasions when our circumstances were particularly uncertain. "Maybe you should go back and live with your father," she would say in our darkest moments together—when she wasn't sure she could continue to care for me. I had a certain curiosity about what it would be like to live with him and Emitsa. What would their home be like? What might my life be like with them?

We later received word that my father was again under house arrest, where he remained until he died in 1972. For twelve years, he was under house arrest, forced to work full-time for the government he despised. My mother later painted a portrait of him under house arrest as she imagined he would appear: a gray-haired, lonely man standing at a window, looking from the inside out.

Part of the pain of losing my father was the realization that living with him was no longer an option. He was dead, and with his death the opportunity for me to live a different life than the one I was living perished, too.

When he was alive, my mother made me write a letter to my father at least once a year, even though I never heard back from him in response. In his absence, I sometimes wondered if he even went to prison when my mother was pregnant with me. I would think, "What if he just left us? Maybe Mama just told me he went to prison so I wouldn't get mad." If he never went to prison, my young mind reasoned, he must have just left us because he didn't care. My thoughts tortured me, never knowing exactly what had happened.

I would write a couple of sentences to my father then dutifully hand off the letter to my mother to mail. It was like writing to a stranger. Sometimes I included a picture or two of myself. This was how my half-brother, Petar, found out about me.

* * *

MY FATHER and Emitsa had a son named Petar, who was six years older than I was. Throughout his childhood and into his teens, he never knew I existed. Because my father was under house arrest, my mother mailed my letters to his home, where he kept a small office. One day Petar happened across one of my letters and saw my photo inside.

Our resemblance was undeniable.

Petar, then about seventeen years old, sent my letter back to me in an envelope with a personal note from him explaining how he had accidentally found out about me. We began a secret correspondence.

I remember the first photo he sent was a picture of himself in a basketball uniform. His eyes were striking and he had a handsome face. I felt an immediate bond with him. He was the sibling I always longed to have. Eventually, my family found out about our letter writing. They arranged for me to meet my brother in Belgrade, where my grandmother lived and Petar was enrolled in school.

It was the first and only time I ever visited my grandmother. I was about eleven years old, and so far I'd failed to display any promise of the social breeding my grandmother thought children my age should have. My mother had always wanted to have a boy. She dressed me in little boy's clothing and had my light-colored hair shaped into an uncomely crew cut. I look like a little boy in the few photographs I have of my childhood. In each one, I'm either playing with balls or standing near a bicycle.

There is, however, one photograph of me in a red dress with longer hair, cradling a baby doll. I don't remember why, but there were occasions when I had to live with other people, whom I knew as my relatives, for short periods. The woman I called my aunt (but probably wasn't) let my hair grow out and had the frilly dress made for me. Of course, the doll wasn't mine; it was simply a prop my "aunt" had borrowed from the photographer.

To my grandmother, my lack of manners and the finer graces was deplorable. The way she talked about me, one would have thought I was raised by wolves. She certainly must not have expected much, since I was my mother's daughter. Still, she made it her personal mission that summer to tame my ways and groom me into being socially acceptable to her friends.

Still, she did not attempt to conceal her disapproval. Whenever she introduced me, she would say, "This is Sasha, Kacha's daughter—you know, the rebellious one." Not knowing any better, I took this as a compliment of sorts and smiled in response to the attentive stares. I assumed my grandmother meant to recognize our adventurous spirit, a title that I was happy to accept at the time. Only later did I realize it was actually intended as insult.

To make matters worse, my aunt Koka's daughter, Dragana, was living there that summer. "Gina," as they called her, was a miniature replica of Koka and Sida at five years old. She looked like a living doll in her ruffled dress and matching bloomers—all gifts from her rich grandfather who owned a nylon stocking factory in Milan, Italy.

I had never seen such feminine, carefully-coordinated outfits like the ones my cousin wore. Something about her and her aura of perfection made me so angry and jealous I wanted to hurt her.

To my embarrassment, I recall taking my cousin Gina behind the apartment building one day and spanking her hand with a long silver spoon until it turned blue. The spoon was the kind that we used to scoop yogurt out of long, skinny-necked bottles. I hit her hard, but I told her to say we were just playing and not to cry. She didn't. Not once. Afterwards, I was so ashamed and saddened by what I had done. It was my way of lashing out against the unfairness in our family, but my actions had been pointless and cruel.

When I arranged to meet my brother, my grandmother had an inexpensive skirt made for me for the occasion. I did not own a single dress, much less a skirt. On the day I was to meet him, I dutifully donned the pleated blue skirt as ordered. I tugged at its uncomfortable waistline and looked at myself in the mirror. My grandmother's efforts proved half-hearted at best. The material she chose was so cheap and easily wrinkled it looked to me as if a cow had been chewing it.

When Petar came to our apartment, he knocked at the front door. Inside, I peered at him through the thick, opaque glass in the door just before I opened it. Through the shadows of the glass, I could see he was holding some sort of yellow flowers. I quickly smoothed my skirt once more, flung open the door, and without so much as a glance toward his face, I threw my arms around his neck. We hugged each other closely. With my grandmother's permission, he took me to his one-room loft nearby where we talked for the next few hours. As I stood before him, Petar took one full-length look at me in my ghastly skirt and laughed aloud.

"I'm going to iron your skirt for you, Sasha," he said decidedly.

I was so ashamed. Here I was meeting my brother for the first time and my appearance was so pitiful it was distracting.

He kindly offered me his robe to put on while he expertly ironed my skirt on a little table.

I thought about how mortified Sida would have been had she observed Petar ironing my new outfit. My grandmother, who had never left her bourgeoisie background behind, would never have gotten over that.

I was glad she wasn't there.

It became a cherished memory my newfound brother and I shared, and one I never forgot. Twenty years would pass before I would see Petar again.

* * *

AS A CHILD, my mother had rebelled against the way she was treated at home. She dreamed of escaping to another life. One day, her mother announced she was sending Kacha to live with her grandfather, Svetislav Stanich, who lived three hundred miles away in Kragujevac.

This was not the first time Sida had sent Kacha away. Once before, when Kacha was four or five years old, Sida had sent her away to a French convent for a year after the sudden death of her husband, who was brutally murdered. Boris Maksimovich, my grandfather, had been a well-respected judge. He first met my grandmother when he was working for her wealthy family, chopping wood to work his way through law school.

Where others may have seen a struggling student, Sida saw in him the potential to advance socially as the wife of a young lawyer. They married after he completed his law degree, and the young couple began a family. Although Sida made little attempt to hide the fact that she had married Boris for his title and not necessarily for love, they lived rather amiably together. Boris quickly moved up in the ranks and became an influential judge in their community. He had always been an art lover, and now that he had the means to collect, he pursued his interests in Italian marble sculptures and many valuable paintings. I was told by my family that in later years, long after the family had moved, their house was confiscated by the regime and served as one of Tito's summer homes.

As judge, my grandfather later presided over a controversial criminal case where the defendant was convicted and sentenced to prison. However, this man had two older brothers who were intent on avenging their baby brother. One day they attacked Boris on a road near a village called Cherry and murdered him. (Ironically, my grandfather never even liked cherries!)

Sida suddenly became a wealthy widow with a new baby and young child at home. A child whose face reminded her so much of Boris that she could hardly look at her. Amidst this tragedy, Sida sent my mother away to live among the Daughters of Charity ("Flying Nuns" who wore white-winged cornettes) so she could deal with her loss and overwhelming sadness on her own while caring for her baby, Koka.

Although the convent was in Yugoslavia, the sisters spoke French. Kacha's young, agile mind quickly absorbed their language, and she learned her prayers in French. On quiet evenings, the sisters often debated among themselves if Kacha's mother would ever return for the young girl or if she would end up staying with them.

After a long year apart, Kacha rejoined her mother and baby sister, but sending her eldest daughter away became a pattern Sida repeated whenever things became too difficult at home. She looked for ways to get rid of Kacha in order to lessen the tension between them. As a teen, Kacha spent the greater part of a year with her grandfather Svetislav—and several summers as well.

Kacha clung to her grandfather Svetislav, who adored her. She was his little girl until the day he died. There in the safety of his home, she could do no wrong. That's not to say she wasn't mischievous. As a child, she once decorated their living room with stripes from three colored pencils she ran chest-high along the walls. Another time, Kacha felt sorry for the family rabbits shivering outside in their cages in the cold winter air. She gathered up the grateful creatures in her arms and let them loose to hop about inside the warm house.

Kacha and Svetislav remained close even after she was an adult. I remember going to visit Svetislav for the first time as a young girl. A few weeks before I was born, he was struck blind. He was cutting wood when a stray chip hit his eye. The white membrane covering his eye fascinated me as a child. I wanted to touch it with my finger and remove it. I always thought it was strange that although only one eye was injured, he became blind in both. Later in medical school, I learned there is such a thing as sympathetic blindness, where the uninjured eye loses vision as well.

My mother named me "Svetislava" after him. "Svet-i-slava" translates as world-and-glory, the combination of the words for *world* (svet) *and* (i) *glory* (slava). In a sense, Kacha found her world in the love of her grandfather—a sanctuary of peace and love where she could be herself and find acceptance. However, at the end of each stay, she would have to return home. Back to the humiliating world of starched white tablecloths where nothing she did was ever good enough for her mother.

Kacha's only advantage over her younger sister was her intellect. When they were older, their mother sent both girls to a prestigious women's business academy. Kacha excelled in her studies, while Koka struggled along. It irked Sida to realize the Kacha would always be a little bit smarter than her younger sister. And Kacha never let Koka forget it.

The competition between the two sisters lasted throughout

adulthood. Koka married a high-ranking official in the Communist party, something my mother considered worse than becoming a prostitute. Part-Italian, his father was the nylon stocking factory owner in Milan who showered their daughter Gina with gifts. They lived an inordinately wealthy lifestyle that was beyond Sida's wildest dreams for her daughter. The irony of the family's lavish homes and yacht in an era of communism, where everyone is supposed to be equal, was not lost on my mother. A sworn enemy of the state, my mother and I were sometimes more afraid of our own family members than we were of strangers on the street.

Sida never remarried after the death of my grandfather. However, a wealthy quarry owner from Romania (who was 24 years her senior) had more or less played a stepfather role in my mother's life. Mihailo Nestorovich, also a noted orator, took a special interest in my mother as a child, and she often traveled with him to his speeches. He developed my mother's interest in art and they would often talk about different paintings and painters while traveling to his speaking engagements.

An art collector himself, he encouraged Mama's budding interest in art and drawing. He told her to always paint, but warned that she must have a profession, too. She took his advice and painted volumes of drawings throughout her entire life, beginning when she was very young. No surface was safe from her constant doodlings and drawings. The backs of papers, envelopes and pieces of wood—virtually any flat surface had the potential to become her next canvas. Once, some pages of an important speech Nestorovich was working on went missing, but he soon discovered they had fallen victim to Mama's hobby. Intricate sketches of birds and a menagerie of insects now lined the margins and backs of his pages. He might have reconsidered his support of Mama's talents right then if he were not so fond of her.

In our family photos, Nestorovich always has a starched white scarf pressed around his neck. His habit after expending himself in delivering a rousing speech was to sit down and enjoy an ice-cold beer. My family became concerned about his beer-drinking routine when Nestorovich suddenly became very hoarse. His brother, a doctor, soon diagnosed him with neck cancer and treated him with radiation. Of course, in those days radiation therapy practices were not as controlled as they are today and there was much more room for error.

Some thought Nestorovich inadvertently received an un-usually high dosage of radiation, because he developed a deep wound in his neck that oozed blood whenever he coughed. He paid a girl to constantly wash and change his scarves through-out the day. The cancer and hole in his neck devastated his ability to deliver speeches. Although he and my grandmother were close, they never married and eventually grew apart.

When Sida developed Parkinson's late in life and could no longer care for herself, Koka coldly relegated her mother to a nursing home far out of the city and rarely visited her. As an adult, I later helped move Sida into another facility nearer to Koka, thinking that she would be better able to look after her mother if she were closer.

Koka and her family never once came to visit her. It broke Sida's heart.

I don't have a single picture of my grandmother where she does not look as though she were going to a party. Her hair is neatly coiffed, her make-up perfect. Even in her last years, she retained that bourgeoisie air about her—regal and dignified to the end.

CHAPTER THREE

HOW BRIGHT
THE STARS

I N THE MIDST OF ALL THE CHAOS OF MY CHILDHOOD, ONE kind and gentle face appeared: Selim Hadjiomerovich, called "Chako." Apparently, Chako knew my father. At one time they had served together in the same regiment, and he had found my mother and me somehow. He was small in stature, with dark black hair that was always shiny from the hair cream he put on it. His face was kind, his lips naturally curling into an easy, gentle smile. I felt an immediate bond with Chako the first day he came to our apartment, and I asked my mother, "Please, can he spend the night with us?" Chako did not stay with us that evening, but he was soon visiting on a regular basis.

He became like a father to me—and in many ways like a mother, too. He would play dolls with me, bending down on his hands and knees on the floor so he could be at my level. He worked as a mechanic. Despite the constant grease under his fingernails, his dark-skinned fingers were delicate enough to craft handmade clothes for my doll. So eager to have someone to play with, I tirelessly engaged him in my favorite games. One time, I threw a single slipper off the balcony three or four stories up for Chako to get. He laughed good-naturedly and retrieved it for me—only to see me throw the other one once he returned. Such patience!

He was also a Muslim, which was not acceptable in those

days. His father was an Hoja, a high-ranking Islamic priest, but Chako was uneducated. Despite their differences, he and my mother were close and he lived with us on and off for about five years. After dinner most evenings, he would help me with my homework. Whereas my mother would chide me if I struggled with the assignments, Chako made me feel as if he understood how hard third grade math could be.

"You are smart. You're the product of two smart people. You can figure it out yourself," my mother would insist and return to reading her own books, as she was an avid reader. I much preferred Chako's empathy to my mother's cold reaction to my complaints.

However, Chako had a secret. A dark secret that threatened my idyllic picture of him. He was an alcoholic—a mean drunk. Only later did I realize that part of the reason we were constantly on the move was because of his violent rages. My mother would move us away from him, and Chako would promptly find us again in a neighboring town. He was a laborer, so he could find a job anywhere. Even after we finally separated from him, my mother's fear that Chako would find us kept us from settling in one place too long.

He would apologize and plead for my mother to give him another chance. She would let him back into our lives, only to be shattered and humiliated a few weeks later when the police would find him passed out in the street. He had a knack for causing a terrific scene when he was drunk, which thoroughly embarrassed my mother.

When my mother finally told me the truth about Chako and why he could no longer be with us, I was shocked. I didn't want to believe it. He had never been anything but kind to me—how could such an awful secret hide behind the smile

I'd grown to love? To convince me why we could not see him again, she told me about something that had happened after yet another of their dramatic separations. Chako and my mother had walked together to a nearby spring to talk when suddenly he took her by the arm, pulled her close and hissed, "I don't know what I should do—kiss you or kill you!"

She could smell the liquor on his breath as she shook herself away from him. That evening she reported him once more to the police and we never saw Chako again.

Of all the people I remember from this time in my life, he is the only one whom I've been tempted to look up on the Internet to find out what happened to him. I have two pictures of my entire schooling in Yugoslavia; one of them is with Chako.

When I was in third grade, he came to my school to visit me for parents' day. I'm not certain that Mama even kept up with what grade I was in. I proudly introduced him to my teacher and classmates and told everyone that he was my dad.

In the class photograph taken that day, my bowl-cut blonde hair rests easy on my fair skin and I am already a head taller than my Gypsy teacher. Next to me is a short, smiling, dark-skinned Muslim man. No one believed he was my father for one minute.

* * *

WE MOVED CONSTANTLY, living in various villages, although frankly much of what I remember from that time in my childhood is only a blur. When we moved, we would simply gather up what belongings we could and close the door behind us. I followed my mother blindly—and looking back, I never felt unnecessarily afraid, nor did I worry about where we were going. I just trusted my mother and clung to her to provide a measure of stability in our lives.

One of the last places my mother and I lived before we immigrated to Austria was the small chrome-mining village of Radusha in Macedonia, near the capital of Skopje. A terrible earthquake in 1963 killed over 1,000 residents and destroyed nearly 80 percent of the entire town, including my school. They placed all of the students in other nearby schools, and I ended up in a primarily Muslim school. Like most children that age, the students didn't particularly want strangers at their school who were nothing like them and did not respect their religious traditions. I instantly became a target for their resentment. More than once, kids beat me up behind the school. One time, I mistakenly brought pork sausage in my lunch, which was deeply offensive to the Muslim religious rules that forbade pork. I learned my lesson.

We had always heard there was a big camp in Traiskirchen, Austria, twenty miles outside Vienna, where families could emigrate from all different countries. Many people would leave Yugoslavia as "tourists" to one of the neighboring countries like Austria and never return. Once they arrived there, they could apply to live almost anywhere in the world.

Of course, in order to travel to Austria, one needed a passport, which we did not have. Mama had been applying for passports for years, long before I was even born, with no success. Each time she applied, they declined her request. The government considered my mother a high-risk person, so she was simply not allowed to travel. Over time, however, Tito's regime grew more and more relaxed, so after eleven years of trying, my mother was finally able to obtain passports for both of us. That's when we made our move.

We took a train across Yugoslavia from Macedonia into Slovenia, then across the border into Austria, near Vienna, where we made our way to the camp called Traiskirchen. We toted our belongings, our passports safely tucked in Mama's hand, and arrived at a little guardhouse in front of the camp, which was fenced all the way around. The man at the guard-house spoke to us in German.

"We want to denounce our citizenship," she announced in perfect German, one of several languages she spoke fluently. She promptly handed over the precious documents we had waited so many years to receive. It was a bold move on my mother's part, but it was understood that Austria had to accept you into their country if you denounced your citizenship else-where and surrendered your passport. That moment marked the day Mama and I lost our Yugoslavian citizenship, which I have never regained to this day.

During this exchange in German, I could not understand what Mama and the man were discussing. I peered around him as they spoke, trying to get a glimpse of what my new home would be like. All I could make out were several large, dark, multi-storied buildings and a number of guards. Several other people were standing in line with us. They separated the men from the women and children as a discretionary measure, and left the men in quarantine as they ushered us into another area.

Three thousand people lived inside this encampment, which was more like a miniature city. In our building, the men lived on the fourth floor and the women and children on the other floors. We would live there for the next year, our every move observed by hundreds of uniformed guards.

Immediately, my mother began making connections with

other people about life inside the camp and what we needed to do next. She was like a dog, sniffing out opportunity wherever it was. She was a great study of people and had a unique ability to sense who would be able to help us if we needed it. Within a few days, she had sized up most of the entire camp—residents, guards and officials—and mentally noted their patterns and personalities.

Mama dealt with these people with her own kind of currency, which wasn't necessarily money. She always traveled with books of rare stamps she had been collecting for years from other stamp collectors. She had pen pals all over the world with whom she traded stamps. When necessary, these stamps proved to be very valuable assets she could trade whenever we needed help or information. Upon arriving at the camp, she got out her books of stamps and started showing them to several people. My mother was an engaging talker, always keeping track of how a contact might help us in the future.

In those first few weeks at the camp, I observed other women and children doing heavy labor under the supervision of the guards, but we were assigned much easier tasks like sweeping the hallways and raking leaves.

Looking back, I realize this was no accident. My mother had somehow wielded some degree of influence with those in charge that kept us from sweating in the sun with the others. There were many times like that, I'm sure, where Mama was busy working behind the scenes to protect me and shield me from hardship as much as she could.

One time she even manipulated our way into taking a day trip to nearby Vienna. Of course, officially we were not allowed to leave the camp. No one was. But Mama had targeted one particular guard who worked on Wednesday afternoons.

"Sasha, that is the one. He will let us do something special if we ask," she told me one morning as we were working. I stopped sweeping long enough to look toward the guard with the kind face. My mother made her way over to him and spoke a few minutes. Later that morning, as I was in my room, she rushed back in and herded me into hurrying and getting my things together. We were headed into town.

My mother and I walked along the streets of Vienna, stopping in front of the big picture window of a butcher's shop. Inside, tantalizing links of golden sausage dangled on a string next to huge legs of lamb dotted with parsley. Inside, the store was sparkling clean with long rows of ice-packed meats nestled together. The butchers at the counter wore crisp white aprons and tied strings around the paper packages they handed to customers. I had never seen anything like it. In my country, there was no thought given to presentation. We had general stores where items like shoes and bread were strewn about on a table right next to each other. There was no time wasted making goods appear attractive to the eye. If you needed it, you would buy it regardless.

The camp in Austria was a type of holding pen—a temporary location for people to live and work in until they were able to establish where they wanted to go from there. This gave camp residents time to secure all the necessary paperwork. At this stage, there were still no guarantees we wouldn't be forced to return to Yugoslavia. We were at a crossroads. We could not stay where we were, because Austria served as only a clearinghouse to send immigrants elsewhere. However, each country had its own set of complicated emigration eligibility rules for regulating potential new citizens. First we would have to choose another country where we wanted to live, and then we could begin taking all the steps to fulfill their requirements.

Mama and I spun the globe in our minds while we worked together, considering all our options. We talked a lot about the merits of moving to Australia. Inside the compound, they sometimes showed the refugees informational films about various countries to demonstrate available options. I remember the film about Australia featured a picturesque scene of a family on a hill surrounded by acres and acres of land stretching out toward the horizon, complete with dogs and sheep in the background. And there was wool—Merino wool—that they worked with their hands.

Something about the wide-open spaces of Australia's rugged outback intrigued us. We were enthralled with the idea that you could have as much land as you wanted there. To think they allowed their citizens to fence off huge pieces of their surroundings and declare, "This is my land." Not that we necessarily wanted to do that, but something about this freedom appealed to us. Still, we did not let our attachment to Australia grow too strong, because we learned we could never meet their eligibility requirements for citizenship.

Part of our problem was that my mother and I shared two separate legal names. She was legally a Cardarullo from her previous marriage. However, my father had made sure I carried the name Vukelja. Our papers had these glaring dissimilarities, and my angular face and lighter, straight hair was in stark contrast to Mama's rounded face and olive complexion. Not only that, I was a minor, which meant the signature of both parents was required before I could immigrate to another country like Australia. With these strikes against us, it was impossible to find a country to accept us. "You have to go back," we were told. Mama and I knew we would be forced to return across the border to Yugoslavia, although we could not predict when.

Everyone who was deported back to his or her country left Austria's border by bus, which dropped its passengers off in the fifty-meter neutral zone between Austria and Slovenia (surrounded by guard towers from both countries), so they could change buses. Some refugees in the camp told us that once you were off the bus, you could run back across the neutral zone into Austria. If you managed to cross the Austrian border, they could never deport you again.

However, it was snowing at this time of year and my mother was adamantly against the idea. She was not convinced it was true and was ready with all kinds of elaborate arguments to defend her position whenever anyone in the camp brought it up.

"Who's to say that this zone is so 'neutral' anyway?" she would scoff. Waving her arms, she grew more and more dramatic thinking of the possibilities. "And what if we slipped on the ice and fell? They could shoot us from both sides!" After a few nightmares about this very scenario happening, we decided against that option. However, we needed to figure out what we were going to do soon, because the day was coming when Austrian officials would no longer let us stay.

* * *

DECADES LATER, long after Mama and I moved to America, I met a girl while visiting my father-in-law in a California hospital. She was obviously Slavic and her accent rose above the noise in the hall, grabbing my attention.

"You're Slavic! Where are you from?" I said excitedly after I turned around and found the nearby woman.

"How do you know that?" the woman said, her accent strong and familiar to my ear. "I'm Romanian."

Many Romanians lived in the Austrian refugee camp where Mama and I had lived and we had picked up several phrases from them. Suddenly a Romanian phrase jumped into my mind that I had not thought of in years. "Say, *sase jumătate*," I told the woman.

The words glided off her tongue, and I asked her to spell it for me. She looked at me cautiously as she took out a pen and carefully scrawled the words on a slip of paper. "Why would you ever know that?" she wanted to know.

Sase jumătate. Sase jumătate. As I let the phrase roll around in my head a few times, my mind went soaring back several decades to those days in the Austrian camp. The phrase meant, "Six and a half," the dreaded early morning hour when the officials began selecting people for deportation. Once a month, at 6:30 a.m., officials swept through the camp to deport specific immigrants. Armed with a list of names, they made their rounds, loudly rapping on doors in each hallway and sending everyone into a panic.

Sase jumătate spread among us like a code. Although it was supposed to be once a month on Thursday mornings, *sase jumătate* could happen anytime. We never knew who would be next, so everyone had to be ready, bags packed. Sometimes it occurred two weeks in a row, and sometimes after a sleepless evening, with our bags packed and at the door, the officials mysteriously did not come at all. Rumors that it would happen one day or the next threatened our existence at a moment's notice.

After a year in the camp, with no country to immigrate to,

we knew our time was up. As we feared, they came for my mother and me one morning at half past six and put us on a bus to be deported.

The bus in Austria was nice with comfortable seats. As we boarded, they gave everyone a brown bag with a blood sausage lunch for our journey. However, once they drove us across the border into the 50-meter neutral zone, the bus dropped us off and we transferred to another bus headed for Maribor, a city near Ljubljana, Slovenia.

I was so sick during the second drive. Compared to the pleasant ride from Austria, the Yugoslavia bus had no seats and we all crammed together like cattle, standing up and holding on for dear life. The bus driver was hurtling us through the streets and slamming on the brakes, then jerking into motion again. Everyone inside was a political refugee and he took no concern for us. At this point, I was throwing up what little blood sausage I ate into the little brown bag.

Others on the bus with us asked if we knew anyone in Maribor. We knew no one. My mother, always thinking on her feet, said we knew the famous medical doctors who were brothers. Dr. Laurich had even delivered me, she pointed out proudly. While that was true, we could hardly pass for acquaintances with the doctor, much less friends. He probably would not even remember us, and besides, we would be in Maribor, several miles away from Ljubljana.

A man next to us felt sorry for me and noticed as I struggled to hold my balance and my lunch. He said to my mother, "Here is my name and where I live. My girlfriend is there and she can take you in and help you." I later found out this stranger on the bus was a gigolo and his "girlfriend" was much older than he was.

"The girl can stay for sure, but my girlfriend—she may be jealous of you because you look so much younger than her," he looked at my mother. "She may have a hard time believing we just met on the bus." Mama just nodded and tucked the information into her pocket.

"They won't keep you very long," he continued, referring to the prison that was our final destination. Mama knew they were taking us straight to prison, but because I was a minor they could only hold us for a week or so.

Later, Mama remarked how fortunate it was that I got sick, because if I hadn't we never would have met this man. And if we didn't meet this man, we would not have had a place to go when we were released. She was always looking at things that way, trying to connect the dots.

When the prison officials talked to us, they interviewed Mama and me separately, which terrified me. Fortunately, they assigned us to the same cell. She warned me not to eat the bread because they put a tranquilizer in it to keep the prisoners calm. I didn't plan to eat any of the moldy, damp bread anyway. It smelled like chemicals and stuck to my hands when I touched it.

The water was teeming with black specks and soot and tasted horrific. Sometimes there were other things floating in it, but I didn't know what they were and Mama said not to drink much of it. Each cell had a toilet, but they were always backed up with sewage. The smell made me gag. I prayed that I would not have a bowel movement the whole time I was there.

There was no bed, only a piece of wood on a small incline, designed for discomfort. I would try to curl up to rest, but would constantly wake up because my legs kept sliding down during the night. The room was unbearably cold, and I snuggled next to my mother under a single thin blanket that barely covered me, much less her.

"Sasha, it could be worse," Mama whispered to me in the darkness that first night as we tried to sleep side-by-side on the incline. "Much worse."

From the bits and pieces Mama had told me about her life before I was born, I knew she was right. I felt her rhythmic breathing next to me and tried to focus on it to drown out the noise from the other cells. People were crying and banging things. Neither of us could sleep that night.

The next day, the officials took us from our cell and separated us again. They put me in a little room with a light bulb hanging from the ceiling. At least it was warm underneath that single bulb, and the water they gave us during the interviews was cool and clean. Mama said to drink as much of it as I could whenever they offered it to me.

They repeatedly asked me the same thing about why we left and what we were doing. Every day for seven days, sometimes even twice a day, they ushered us out of our cell and into separate rooms to be interviewed, trying to get information out of us. I answered their questions the best I could. Mama said to tell them that I didn't know where I was going, that I was just following her. They seemed to accept that, but still they hounded me with the same question in different ways repeatedly, hoping to glean some new insight.

Within a few days, some of the guards had taken to me and were calling me nicknames. They called me "Poopie," which meant "little boy," because I wore a plaid cap with a fringed pom pom on top of my short hair. The interrogators were much more serious. They wanted to know why I hated my country so much that I wanted to leave it.

I knew better than to agree that I hated it. The kids in school had taught me that lesson early on. Each child in my class had to wear a bright red scarf around our necks in honor of Tito's regime. We even had to tie it in a certain way. The other children were quick to correct me if I was lazy and let the knot become untied or if I slung it to the side while playing. They tugged at me and harassed me constantly. One day, I was in a hurry, rushing to school, and I forgot my scarf altogether. The others seized me at recess, beating me with their fists and calling me a traitor. "Your mother is not a Communist. Is something wrong with her?" they would tease.

When the interrogators asked me if I hated Tito and what he was doing to our country, I would say nothing to imply that I didn't like him. I knew what they could do to me was much worse than what had happened on the playground.

These interviews soon became like a game to me. If I answered their questions the same way every time, I would get the water and drink. Answer the questions, get the water. Answer more questions, get more water. I learned from my mother to always get something out of every situation, no matter how difficult it was. She showed me how to turn even the worst situations to my advantage.

Mama comforted me by encouraging me to count the days we had left. We knew they could not hold us indefinitely because of my age, so we tried to put our minds elsewhere by focusing on what would happen when we got out. Mama still had the man's name from the bus tucked into her belongings, and she spent each evening building up the story for me.

"We will go to this nice man's house and his girlfriend will already know who we are and take us in. And if that doesn't work out, we still have the famous doctor who delivered you, Dr. Laurich."

I nodded sleepily, trying to find a spot to rest my head on the cold wooden slab. Another door slammed and several people were rustling about. Somewhere nearby I could hear a woman's muffled weeping. These were the night sounds we'd grown halfway used to, but not entirely. Mama just ignored the commotion and carried on with her plans.

"See, Sasha? Everything is going to work out. Not only do we know one person, we know two now! We have so much to do. We just have to get out of here."

Mama was an optimist if she was anything. Except for one time, I never knew her to lose hope. There was always something that could work out. Later in life, she would qualify that she was "not a pessimist, but a well-informed optimist." So much had happened by then that I understood how she felt. Even so, I never thought of her as a pessimist. Some might say the way she plowed through our adversity was either instinctively courageous or a reflection of her total lack of a grasp on reality. Either way, she was determined to make life better. When she saw our future, she didn't see how bleak the darkness, only how bright the stars.

SEEDS

CHAPTER FOUR

MY JESUIT BROTHERS

MAMA ALWAYS TOLD ME I WOULD GO TO SCHOOL AND get an education. Everyone in my family was educated, so that was a given. The only question remaining was what I would become. A professor? Perhaps follow my parents and get my doctorate in Economics? Or maybe I would decide to become a doctor, a vocation Mama supported, as long as I didn't have to "handle the secretions."

The prospect of my becoming a doctor and working with other people's urine and saliva horrified my mother. In the future, when I graduated from medical school, my mother cried alongside the other mothers in the audience, but they likely mistook her sobs as tears of happiness over my accomplishment.

I knew better.

She was still coming to terms with the fact that her brilliant only child was, in fact, occasionally going to deal with excrement. However, my mother had an interest in medicine and always kept a home medical reference book nearby so she could flip through the pages and look up information about random diagnoses.

She even self-diagnosed her malaria when we were living in Macedonia. I remember a recurring fever that would rack her body with violent rigors for several days in a row. Then the symptoms would pass, and for several months she would be fine. When her fever was the highest, she would often hallucinate, talking in great detail about the imaginary baby chicks under her bed. I was seven years old and feared my mother must have mental problems.

I slept on the floor next to her during these episodes but still heard the iron-frame bed creaking with her incessant shaking. The first time it happened, she suddenly nudged me awake.

"Go move the chicks, they've escaped!"

She was sitting straight up in bed, the sheets a damp and tangled knot, staring at the empty corner of our room and fervently pointing at yellow baby chicks that were not there. I hesitated a moment, blinking my eyes and squinting at the corner.

"Sasha, do as I say," she ordered, her gaze unmoving.

I scampered to the corner and flapped my arms trying to shoo the "chicks" back underneath her bed. I did this three or four times throughout the night and into the next morning. A doctor later confirmed my mother's self-diagnosis and noted that she had all the symptoms of malaria, including very high fever and visual hallucinations. I was relieved to know my mother was not crazy—she just had malaria.

* * *

HOWEVER DIM the light was before us, Mama could always make out the faint shape of my future. She kept that hopeful dream before me, and I never questioned that we would make it out of prison and eventually out of Yugoslavia.

It was no surprise to me that Mama was right once again when the guards opened our cell door a week later and told us we were free to go, just as she had said. Not free to go anywhere far, of course. But then again, we didn't have anywhere to go other than the apartment belonging to the girlfriend of the man we had met on the bus. And she was, in fact, nice to me, as the man had promised. However, we would soon discover that this woman's open hospitality extended only to me.

*　*　*

IT WAS LATE in the afternoon and the sun was already beginning to set when we arrived at the girlfriend's apartment. She opened the door a crack, and I could tell from the lines on her face that she was nearly twice as old as my mother was. She had on a faded housecoat and little black slippers. Her gaze fell to me first, and her eyes crinkled as she smiled a gray-toothed little smile. She had been expecting us.

Then her eyes darted toward my mother and her expression changed entirely. She was suspicious because her boyfriend had sent us there. He was apparently a kept man, and this older woman who was caring for him felt threatened at the slightest provocation. My mother, though not a beauty, was obviously younger and prettier than the tired woman peering at us through the partially open door. She began quizzing my mother, still undecided if she would let us in.

"Come in," she finally determined after several long minutes, squinting at my mother as if silently issuing a dare. We squeezed past her as she leaned against the doorframe, still uncertain that we were who we said we were.

We spoke for a few minutes more and she warmed up to us. She was nurturing toward me right away, and I began to like her. However, she matter-of-factly said to my mother, "I could take care of your child, but you cannot stay."

The finality in her voice frightened me. What did this nice

lady mean, my mother could not stay? However, Mama did not seem too put off by this, and we ended up staying for the light meal the woman served us—our first meal out of prison.

After dinner, Mama kissed me on the cheek and told me she would spend the night somewhere else and come for me in the morning. There was something in my mother's eyes that I'd never seen before. Something dead. It sent cold chills through me as she walked out the door. The night air surrounded her silhouette as I watched her make her way down the street, clutching the suitcases that contained all our earthly belongings.

I had no idea where she was going or what would happen to me in this stranger's house. Once again, I felt blind trust and assurance that Mama would figure something out. I never doubted that she would come back for me. As a mother myself, I now know the anguish she must have felt leaving me there. But something else was going on with Mama that I did not realize at the time. Years later, she told me about what happened during what she said was the darkest night of her life.

Mama had left the woman's flat and walked aimlessly until she reached a train track running through Maribor. She walked along the tracks, contemplating if it wouldn't be better if she just threw herself underneath the next train. For her to think that way was very contrary to her natural personality. She'd always been incredibly brave, full of life and hope. Now the weight of our situation rested fully on her—so heavy it nearly smothered her.

She reached a small church near the tracks and wandered in to pray. It was a very Austrian-looking church with a sloping roof and soaring walls. Slovenia and Austria are so similar in terms of culture and architecture that they're even called

Yugoslav-Austria. My mother settled into one of the carved wooden pews at the back. By this time it was late at night. A cleaning lady was busy polishing one of the railings near the front and did not notice my mother come in.

"What kind of church is this?" my mother asked quietly, her voice echoing through the empty chamber.

The woman said the priests were Jesuits.

A Catholic church, Mama thought to herself, her brow tightly furrowed. "Can I talk with a priest?" The woman left her post and went through a doorway to the left to find the priest.

My mother planned to tell the priest how upset she was with the Catholic Church. Their refusal to annul her earlier marriage to Nino had hopelessly complicated our emigration options and now we had nowhere to go.

Soon a man with a kind face, wearing a long dark robe and triangular-shaped hat, came in and walked toward my mother. He said his name was Father Cobi, and he sat down next to her. As she spoke to him, she clutched a well-worn plastic bag that contained all our legal documents. Her birth certificate (as well as mine), her certificate of marriage to Nino and other gently folded legal documents were all crammed into this bag, which she never let out of her sight. She carried it with her everywhere, every day of her life.

She began explaining her entire story. How she had lived with her mother and sister in Belgrade and had married an Italian in a Catholic church. How she was a political refugee and had given birth to me in Ljubljana. How we had traveled as far as Austria but couldn't stay because we didn't meet the emigration criteria of any other countries.

And now she had just gotten out of prison, and her daughter was staying with a stranger whose boyfriend we had met on the bus. All the while, Father Cobi never said a word. He just listened intently as she went on and on. When she was through explaining, he asked only one question.

"Can I see your wedding certificate?"

Mama thought that was strange. Out of everything she'd told him, why this request? Nevertheless, she dug through the bag until she found the document and carefully unfolded it to show the priest. He held the creased paper in his hands and looked at it carefully. He never looked at Mama, only the document.

That made Mama nervous. Convinced he had not understood a single word she'd said, she started to take the piece of paper back from him and leave. Just then he spoke. So quiet was his voice that she had to lean in to hear what he was saying.

"It's my..." he began, shaking his head slowly.

She leaned in further as he continued.

"It's my signature at the bottom of this certificate."

He looked up into Mama's eyes at that point. They both stared at each other for a brief moment, and then Father Cobi broke out into a small smile.

Mama smiled, too. Twenty years ago, in a church halfway across the country from Maribor, Father Cobi had been the priest who married two young lovers, Kacha and Nino Cardarullo, when my mother was eighteen.

"You're welcome to come here and stay with us. And bring your baby, too," he offered, gently squeezing her hand reassuringly. She had been talking to him about her "baby" and wondering how she could care for her. At fourteen, I was hardly an infant, which the Jesuit brothers soon discovered a few hours later when I showed up on their doorstep with the "poopie" hat still on my head.

They took us to a woman on their compound who housed missionaries, and she offered us a room in her small apartment. The modestly furnished place was on the third floor and overlooked the church. She served us bowls of hot soup, and I swore I had never tasted anything so good.

"I'm sorry there is only one bed," the woman apologized after she showed us to our room. She turned down the covers and snapped on the lamp on the bedside table.

The small, metal-framed bed with clean sheets and soft blanket tucked in around the edges seemed indulgent to us, compared to where we had been sleeping the past week, and we assured her it was fine. Mama and I appreciated this much-needed night's rest, since early the next day we would join the other priests and brothers at the church and go to work.

* * *

MAMA WAS Greek Orthodox, but at this time not really practicing by any means. To her, this coincidence with Father Cobi was a matter of destiny or fate. It felt right to both of us, as if we were meant to be there.

I remembered three years earlier, before we left Yugoslavia, a petite Gypsy lady would come and clean our apartment. We didn't call her a cleaning lady, because no one could have one of those in a Communist country. When she finished working, the Gypsy lady would sit with my mother and they would drink Turkish coffee together, followed by a bit of fortune-telling. The tradition of interpreting the shapes left behind in a finished cup of the thick brew is as least as old as Turkish coffee itself.

After the drink is finished, the cup is turned upside down on the saucer and left to cool. The muddy mixture of grounds slowly runs down the sides of the cup and dries, leaving much to the imagination as to what the various streaks and shapes indicate about future relationships, illnesses and events. One day after the Gypsy lady and Mama had shared their two cups of coffee, she turned Mama's cup to peer inside and a strange look came onto her face.

"I see a lot of men in black robes..." she began and turned the cup toward the light to get a better view.

"They're walking around in a garden."

"Men? Are you sure they're men?"

"Yes, they're men. But I don't know what they're doing."

Mama shrugged and began brewing more coffee, entirely forgetting about the incident until years later, when we found ourselves in the company of the Jesuits. One day, Mama called me to the window. A group of Jesuits with long, dark, flowing robes were pacing the garden in silent prayer inside the courtyard. "Look!" she pointed to the men, her voice quivering with excitement. "Men in black robes walking in a garden." The same mysterious scene the Gypsy woman had seen years ago.

St. Ignatius of Loyola and six other students at the University of Paris founded the Jesuits in the 1500s. Bonded by vows of chastity and poverty, these young men formed a brotherhood devoted to charitable work throughout Italy. It has grown into the largest male order of the Roman Catholic Church. Their kindness is legendary, as is their dedication to God's service, through their schools and mission work. Just miles away from that horrific prison, we found refuge among these kind Jesuits. We had seen the best and the worst in people, two bookends of human nature, all in the same week and within the same city walls, mere miles apart.

The next day, when we awoke, we went back to the church. As expected, they wanted us to earn our keep right away. Everyone there, priests and brothers included, worked diligently with their hands to do something useful and beneficial.

They asked Mama what she could do. Her PhD in Economics did not prove to be very useful in this setting. She could barely type. She'd never needed to learn, because her assistant did her typing at work. She considered herself an avant-garde housekeeper, which simply meant she never cleaned. When Mama died, I found three aprons she had bought in flea markets, all unused. But the Jesuits had a philosophy that you eat only if you work. At the end of every day, you had to show what you had accomplished that day.

Mama ended up doing everything—everything she hated. Every day over the next year, she sewed, darned socks and even learned to type announcements and Mass schedules by pecking out one letter at a time on a rickety keyboard. Just when she finished one chore, the brothers assigned her another—from washing their robes to ironing the starched white lace they wore over their robes for Mass. When summoned, Mama trudged into the church after Mass to collect the challises and polish every piece of silver and gold until her fingers throbbed and the candlesticks gleamed.

Although they only served one meal a day as a reward for all your hard labor, it was no more than they ate. After dinner, Mama and I would walk home, exhausted but content, back to the woman's apartment where we were staying. Sometimes in the evenings, the brothers showed reel movies on a wrinkled white sheet they pinned on a wall. These grainy short films depicted the lives of various saints in history. At first, I wasn't sure what to expect, but I soon began anticipating these stories, eager to watch them over and over again.

Afterwards, the brothers would quiz us about the saints' lives and we would talk about their sacrifice to serve others. Of course, what we saw on the film was no different from how the Jesuits we knew lived every day. The Jesuit brothers had few possessions and only a few pieces of simple stick furniture in their rooms. They owned only two shirts, one to wear while the other was in the wash. I never before saw anyone work as hard as they prayed and pray as hard as they worked.

The brothers gave me prayer cards as gifts—beautiful, small colored drawings of different saints with prayers on the backs. I took the delicate treasures home and put them inside a book I kept in our room. At night, I would mull through my collection by lamplight, staring at the saints' faces and wondering who they were and why they lived the way they did.

Mama had told me about one of our relatives, John Maximovich (he spelled his name with an "x"), who was a highly regarded Serbian Orthodox bishop in the mid-1900s. She often showed me his filigree, a necklace made of tightly woven silver threads, along with a postcard picture she had of him. "He was a holy man, Sasha, in *our* family," she would say proudly. He had an unusual ability to pray around the clock, pausing only to rest for brief periods in his "bed" that was actually just a chair. He visited the sick night and day and served in St. Petersburg, Shanghai and the Philippines before immigrating to America, where he served at a church in San Francisco until he died in 1966. In 1994, I was privileged to attend his glorification ceremony, where he was honored as a saint. In fact, it was a friend of my mother's from Brussels who contacted me and urged me to attend. "Your mother would have walked to California to witness this moment," she noted.

The elaborate ceremony lasted for three days, with all-night vigils and various processions. I had to look in Mama's bag and bring our birth certificates with me to San Francisco in order to be admitted as a family member among the throngs of thousands of people in attendance, which included a professional film crew. I met family members I never knew I had, and I felt a kinship with this holy man who had spent his life helping others.

When I learned about Father Damien's work with leprosy patients on the island of Molokai in Hawaii during the 1800s, something about his compassion for the least members of society moved me. He had gone to Hawaii as a missionary, serving the Hawaiian people who were plagued by many new diseases like syphilis and influenza that foreign traders and sailors had inadvertently introduced to the natives.

Leprosy was one of the most devastating of these illnesses, so much so that the Hawaiian king banished infected men, women and children to a quarantined area behind a mountain ridge on a remote island. Father Damien was assigned to the Catholic mission nearby. He eventually requested to serve the colony itself, to live and serve among them until he too died from leprosy.

I could not understand the depth of his love that drove him to seek what some called a "death sentence" among these people who were so gruesomely disfigured. Outcasts of society, they had become nearly wild. His story fascinated me, with his tireless efforts to build schools and turn what was a shantytown into a sustainable community. I can trace the first desire I had to become a physician to these summer evenings when I learned about Father Damien and others like him.

In many ways, as a cancer doctor I feel a certain kinship with Father Damien and his work with lepers. Cancer has become the leprosy of the modern age. Society is scared of this unruly disease that ravages the human body. It can be every bit as disfiguring as leprosy, as patients have pieces of their body removed bit by bit in an effort to heal. Patients undergoing treatment are often isolated to receive their chemotherapy and radiation and feel strikingly alone in their experience. In the old days, once someone got cancer, life was over—much like it was for those who contracted leprosy. Patients literally went home to die. Today, leprosy is no longer a threat due to effective treatments, and we're working to eradicate cancer likewise.

My dream of being a physician was born while I sat in the darkness of that little room, watching the documentaries of the priests. It was a secret I kept to myself for many years. I did not want anyone to spoil it for me and tell me how foolish it was for a refugee to dream something like that. So I told no one.

When I wasn't working alongside Mama, dusting statues and ironing to earn my meals, I spent two to three hours in school every day in order to keep up with my education. I had also found a new focus in my life. Not yet knowing how to maintain balance whenever something new was introduced to me, I became almost pathological about it. Every day I would go into the church by myself to pray and meditate for hours at a time, sometimes even two or three times a day. I memorized a number of prayers in Latin and repeatedly mouthed them onto the face of the stone floor beneath me. Even though I did not understand their full meaning because they were in Latin, I felt drawn to prayer in ways I could not explain.

I knelt on the cold, cobblestones for so long that I was in

pain by the time I would get up to go back to my room. I don't know exactly what I was praying about all the time, but I remember that I found such peace in those quiet moments alone.

It felt as though wave upon wave of cleansing rain washed over me. Even Mama didn't understand the urgency of my need to go to church. She went to Mass on Saturdays and Sundays, but she could find me there any day of the week. I had never been to church before and had never heard about Jesus Christ or any of the other fascinating stories.

In my country there were Greek Orthodox churches, but the only ones who attended were old people with haggard faces who dressed in black. I had never seen young people in church before now, but many of the Jesuit brothers were vibrant young adults who liked to sing upbeat songs.

I was thrilled when Father Svoljshak, who was younger than Father Cobi, offered to baptize me. My mother decided she would also convert to Catholicism because she wanted to be of the same faith as her child. When most children are baptized into the Catholic Church, their godparents are then informally responsible for them, making sure their religious education, for example, is carried out.

Father Svoljshak believed we also needed someone to come alongside of us who could help us. Since we knew no one outside the church, he chose my godparents for me, hoping they would help us financially. He knew an older half-Austrian couple, the Schmidts, who had lost both of their twin sons, one to appendicitis and one a week later in an inexplicable coincidence. They had a house in Austria and lived in Yugoslavia, which made me wonder if I might somehow end up back in Austria.

At my baptism, they gave me a gold chain with a heart,

cross and anchor to represent faith, hope and love. But otherwise they were very cold toward me, which was due more to their Austrian upbringing than anything else. I'm not sure what Father Svoljshak's plan was, but it didn't work out, because the Schmidts faded out of the picture.

We would remain with the Jesuits for the rest of the year. Mama processed our experience among the Jesuits in a different way than I did, but she could see how deeply it affected me. I could not get enough of this mysterious new world into which we had somehow stumbled. The Jesuits introduced Mama to St. Jude, the patron saint of lost causes. Apparently, St. Jude had an affinity for people in desperate situations, something she took to right away.

If anyone needed a miracle, it was Mama. Yet just when we thought our miracle was taking root, the winds changed and scattered the seeds once again.

* * *

IN THE CLOISTER (from the Latin word *clausura*, which means "to shut up"), the brothers safeguarded their vows of celibacy from worldly temptations. One day the younger brothers unhinged the doors and window frames in the little enclave of rooms where they lived and brought them down to us to paint. It was forbidden to have a young girl like me in the brothers' rooms. They simply brought the work to us in the courtyard. Mama and I did the work of several men, scrapping off the chunks of old, flaking paint and sanding down the surface until it was smooth. Then we gave the windows and doors a fresh new coat of paint.

While we were finishing the last doors, Padre Arupe, who

was known as their Black Pope, came to visit the church from Portugal. Black Pope was the nickname for the Father General of the Jesuits, named so because of the black priestly robe he wore, in contrast to the Pope's white robes. He saw me working with Mama in the courtyard and darted his eyes at Father Cobi and Father Svoljshak. When he met with them privately, he expressed his shock that they allowed a young teenage girl to live and work among young novices who were still in their initial training and proving period before their acceptance as priests.

"The mother can stay, but not the girl. That is too much temptation for the young novices. Take care of this within the week," he sternly ordered Father Cobi.

Even then, he was making an exception to allow my mother to stay. I suppose she was older and less of a temptation to the young men. As for me, I was still a tomboy at heart, so it never occurred to me that there might be something potentially sinful about my presence among my Jesuit brothers.

It was true that most of the guests who would stay in the missionary quarters where we lived had always been men— other Jesuits traveling through and only staying a short while at the monastery. Father Cobi had made a huge exception to allow us to stay there that long.

At this time, although we had not come to them as believers, the church had been at the helm of our lives, directing our path for over a year. It was one of many times when neither Mama nor I felt as if we were in control—things were just coming together on their own. Our lives were caught up in the current of a swift river that twisted and turned, spilling us haphazardly into the unknown future waiting around the bend. Sometimes the unpredictability and speed with which things happened were terrifying. Then there were periods when the rapids would subside, breaking into long stretches of calm—like our time in Austria, and the year with the Jesuits, where we had time to rest and think about our future.

I realize now that my mother made some decisions on sheer impulse, but the river's current ensured we always tumbled forward somehow. We could not fight against it or go back to any previous point. If we had tried, we would have exhausted ourselves with the effort and might even have lost our lives along the way. Certain decisions Mama made cancelled out other options, but many times the decisions seemed like they were made for her. It was otherwise impossible to explain all the places we ended up. With few exceptions, it was never what my mother would have imagined for us, but she saw it as the next step in the plan.

Such was the case when Father Svoljshak sent a message to his five sisters, all nuns, who worked like horses and lived together amid rolling green hills in the shadow of the Austrian Alps. His message had one simple request: Did they have room for two more?

Section Two
CHAPTER FIVE

THE KINDNESS
OF STRANGERS

MANY PEOPLE CARED FOR MY MOTHER AND ME THROUGH-
out my childhood. Their names I can no longer remember, but their faces are unforgettable. They are all strangers who share nothing more in common than a kind word or a
warm touch in my memory.

I remember we once spent the night in the home of a Seventh Day Adventist family. Some acquaintances had given us
their names. "Just say you know us," they said assuredly, and
that is what we did. We waited patiently outside of their church
to find the family, and with barely so much as an introduction
they took us home with them that afternoon.

We ate dinner together at their table, and they amica-
bly seated me beside their other children. That evening they
tucked us into the bed where their youngest daughter usually
slept. The room was cozy and quiet. There was a brown blanket hanging over the back of a wooden chair in one corner and
a small stack of the little girl's toys in another.

On the windowsill was a small kitchen cup filled with
dirt and the first green shoots of a tiny plant poking through
the soil. It was probably something the little girl had made in
school and brought home. I touched my finger lightly to the
top of the soil and ran it across the delicate shoot of the plant.
Because we had not yet been rooted anywhere for any length
of time, Mama and I had not had the chance to grow. Our lives

had so far remained only seeds, dark and formless shapes scattered from one place to the next.

I suppose we all begin life that way, with the insignificance of a handful of seeds. We carry our potential in a delicate balance of hopes and dreams that either take root or are trampled underfoot. Seeds, like dreams, remain dormant in the darkness beneath the soil until the right conditions and the right timing come together.

The basic conditions that caused the little seed in the cup to burst its shell and grow seemed to happen only sporadically for Mama and me, if at all. Kindness from a stranger was a summer rain—bringing cool refreshment one moment only to vanish the next. Someone would arrive at just the right moment, gentle gardeners sent to work the soil and nourish hope within us. They would do their part, but then leave as quickly as they had appeared on the scene.

As I went to sleep that evening in the Seventh Day Adventists' home, I thought about how I wouldn't mind staying there, in that home with this family. I almost woke Mama up to ask her if we could stay. However, by morning we were gone, on our way to the next destination—somewhere only Mama knew. This constant uprooting repeated itself many, many times.

* * *

WITHIN the week, we heard back from Father Svoljshak's sisters that we could come if we promised to work. Father Svoljshak assured them we were fine workers and arranged for our travel the next day to Mojstrana, a sleepy Slovenian village we would call home for the next several months.

I was not necessarily excited about this new place, nor do I remember feeling a sense of adventure or even apprehension when we left the Jesuits. I approached it as I approached each of our moves: It was something we had to do. All of our decisions came with very little feelings attached. Padre Arupe had said we couldn't stay at the convent, so that was that. I don't recall how I felt about the move. That didn't matter. My mother and I were rarely in a position to protest where we lived.

We arrived by train to Mojstrana (which translates as "my side") and the sisters sent for us in an older truck. We brought our suitcases of belongings, including pictures from my baptism and a book about Mother Teresa the Jesuits had given us. My book of saints was full of prayer cards now, each one carefully glued onto a page. Father Svoljshak had even included some handwritten notes near some of the cards. I also carried with me my first copy of the Bible—another gift from the Jesuits that I kept safely folded between my clothes in my suitcase. And, of course, tucked into every crevice of our suitcases were my mother's oil brushes, rolled up canvases and the hope that she could paint. We never left those behind.

Father Svoljshak was careful to build up Mojstrana in my mind as if we were on our way to a resort destination on the Austrian border. Although it was hardly a vacation, with five tireless nuns running the household, the visual feast he had described was true. I rubbed some of the smudged dirt off the truck window with the back of my hand as we traveled to their home and looked out. The beauty of the Julian Alps shadowed endless and lush green fields. Only a few wood-framed homes dotted an almost surreal landscape. Neighbors were spaced far, between each other's fields, lining the three Alpine valleys of Mojstrana.

We drove past several long, narrow sheds that were open on one side. Each one had a shingle roof and thick timbers framing its sides. When we passed, I craned my neck around to look inside and saw several racks holding bunches of hay, left there to dry. I later learned these racks, called hay harps, were part of a traditional drying method in Slovenia for collecting hay. It wasn't long before Mama and I learned how to cut the hay, bundle it and carry it down the mountain to the hay harps to dry.

I remember late afternoons when, after our day's work was done, I would run downhill through the hay fields, running and running until I tumbled, breathless, into the soft stacks to break my fall. Mama painted a lot of scenery in Mojstrana. She too seemed inspired by our happy existence among the peaceful surroundings and, when we weren't working, spent hours capturing it on canvas.

The nuns' modest yellow home was a classic, colorful Austrian alpine style and hardly big enough for the five sisters— much less two new houseguests. We stayed in a common area in the center of the home that housed an upright tiled furnace for heat. We slept next to the stove on a makeshift bed—just a cushioned bench that was slightly wider than normal. At night, I propped my feet against the beautiful decorative tiles surrounding the furnace, tracing their intricate patterns with my toes and soaking in the warmth. It was heavenly! Especially in Yugoslavia, my feet were always cold and wet because decent shoes weren't available. This helps explain why, when I immigrated to America and got a job, I scrimped and saved to buy waterproof boots! I put them on before leaving the store in New York, and headed straight for the first puddle I saw on the sidewalk to test out my purchase. I splashed my boots in the puddle—and my feet stayed toasty and dry. The joy it gave me to have dry, warm feet was just one of a hundred little things that only a non-American could truly appreciate.

The Jesuit brothers worked hard, but these sisters were not to be outdone. From sunup to sundown, we worked the hay fields, resting only at night. Other than our work, we didn't have anything to give the nuns in return for their kindness and hospitality. What these women and other people like them did for us made a deep impression on me. We were new converts to the Catholic faith, and yet we owed the Catholic Church more than we could ever repay.

Decades later, as an adult, it took me a long time to consider changing churches. Not because my identity was rooted in being Catholic, but because I was so loyal and thankful for all that Catholics had unselfishly given us. They were strong links in the chain of people who passed us from one person to the next, to the next. There were times when Mama and I never unpacked. The next morning we would be off again. Even though we stayed in Mojstrana several months, we knew it was another transition point. We could not remain there permanently any more than we could have stayed in the Jesuit monastery.

I had two relatives on my mother's side (whom I referred to as my aunts) who lived in Belgium. Olga Miloradovich was in the Belgian Congo and served as the first forensic pathologist in that area. She and her husband, another forensic pathologist, had five children. The story I always heard about them was that Olga's husband had performed the autopsy on Mike Todd, an American film producer and the third husband of Elisabeth Taylor, after his fatal plane crash. Of course, stories about relatives seem to take on a life of their own, and I have no way of knowing if this is true.

Olga's sister, Milette Miloradovich, lived in Brussels and was a professor in the École des Beaux-Arts ("School of Fine Arts," a system of influential art schools). She was talented and well respected, but eccentric. Mama contacted her to ask if she would sponsor us to come to Belgium. In response, my aunt wrote a letter of guarantee to the Belgium government stating that she would be personally responsible for us if we immigrated to Belgium. By this time, Tito's regime had relaxed its restrictions even more, and we were able to travel to Belgium without delay.

Aunt Milette was a bohemian who loved art and enjoyed an eclectic existence in a beautiful apartment in Belgium. In her letter to us, she raved about city life in Brussels and said how wonderful it would be for us to stay in her luxurious apartment while we looked for our own place to live. She would help me get into the best schools, she assured us, making extravagant promises to care for us. However, Aunt Milette issued her offer under the watchful eye of her boyfriend Freddy, an older man with a sallow complexion who also happened to be a staunch Communist.

When I met Freddy, I couldn't help staring. He looked like Rasputin with his long, curly white hair and unkempt beard that nested in the folds of his hair at his shoulders. He had a copy of a red leather book tucked under one arm, which I noticed he carried with him throughout the evening. I later learned it was a book by Mao Tse-Tung, the Communist leader of China. Freddy seemed to greet Mama with the disinterest of an old dog, and he barely acknowledged me either. He slunk around in the background, finally settling into their bedroom as Aunt Milette flitted about in her excitement over her visitors.

She swept back her dark, unruly hair with one hand, the

whites of her wild eyes rimming the dark circles of her irises. She looked as if she had just woken up and eagerly showed us around her place. It had changed dramatically since she had written her letter to us. There was now hardly any furniture at all, even though she had described her finely appointed furnishings in detail throughout her letter. Mama and I had often talked about Aunt Milette's apartment at length before we arrived, envisioning exquisite wall-to-wall mahogany pieces that could make a heart ache with envy.

On a whim, Aunt Milette had seen a painting she wanted and had gathered up every piece of furniture and put it in consignment in order to buy the painting. The enormous canvas of modern art stretched across one of the bare walls, but the white and black splotches painted by somebody famous meant nothing to me. A grand piano, the only remaining item in the nearly naked room, dwarfed the two tiny camping-style cots she had set up for us. We were so tired from our journey that we politely excused ourselves after supper and collapsed onto our cots.

Freddy had hardly said a word during the meal, but his demeanor hardened more in the hours after we arrived. What I had initially interpreted as his disinterest toward us now seemed to linger between cold dislike and seething anger. Whatever it was that was bothering him, I decided I didn't want to find out.

"I don't like Freddy," I said to Mama in a hushed voice as we dressed for bed in the big room, our suitcases stacked against the broad wooden legs of the piano.

Aunt Milette and Freddy had retired to their bedroom with the door closed.

"Shhhh," Mama sternly warned, looking toward their door

and grazing her finger across her lips.

"He scares me." I tried again, whispering now. Mama didn't have to say anything. I could tell she did not like him either.

I slipped on my pajamas and crawled under the sheet on my cot. I was exhausted and fell into a deep sleep immediately. Suddenly, I felt something cold against my neck and a burst of warm breath wash over my shoulder. I gasped and reached for Mama next to me, so frightened that my throat closed over my words and I could not make a sound. Freddy was standing above us both, moonlight shining through the wisps of his beard. He was holding a knife.

"I know who you are," he growled. He had apparently figured out that we were not just Milette's distant relatives here for a visit. We were political refugees on the lam, running away from people exactly like him. He had the perfect, piercing stare of a madman, with small bubbles of white foam dotting the corners of his mouth.

In an instant, Mama grabbed me by the arm and rolled off the cot, half-dragging me behind her and knocking over our suitcases. We burst through the front door and down the steps onto the nearly deserted street. A cab rounded the corner at that moment, and for reasons I cannot explain, stopped at the insistence of a crazy woman and her child waving their arms clothed only in their pajamas.

"Yugoslav Embassy," she commanded him as we dove into the backseat. All our belongings, with the exception of the bag of documents that Mama never left anywhere, remained behind.

The cab driver took off and Mama leaned her head back against the fake leather headrest and let out a deep breath. We sat in silence for a full minute before she spoke. Tears were streaming down my face, but I was still too shocked to let out a sob. I looked at my mother to see if she was crying. When she spoke, her voice was strong and clear.

"Yugoslavia was bad…but not this bad. These are *crazy* people! I want to go back."

I looked at her blankly, still unable to accept that this was real and not some terrible dream. Mama, seeing the terror in my face, just patted my hand and gave me half a smile before she turned her head from me and stared out the window at the Brussels skyline passing by.

I don't recall ever seeing my mother cry, but I am fairly certain that the moonlight streaming through the window highlighted a small tear rolling down her cheek.

* * *

WE ARRIVED at the Yugoslav Embassy. With the cab driver impatiently waiting to be paid, we approached the doors of the Embassy, which was part of a larger apartment building.

There was no doorbell, so Mama grabbed the thick metal doorknocker and pounded three times. It was the middle of the night. The knocks echoed through the building and down the empty street, so loudly I covered my ears. I thought we were going to wake the entire neighborhood.

No one answered.

Mama knocked again, and this time the door right next to it, Rue de Crayer 11, creaked open. A woman was standing there in the doorway, a pale pink robe tied over her silk nightgown.

"They're not going to answer," she said in a lovely French

accent. She spoke gently, as if she were having tea instead of being rudely awakened by two strangers in the middle of the night.

"They've had some kind of bomb threat this evening and everyone has gone home. Why don't you come in here?"

Her name was Madame Camille Regout, the wife of Pierre Regout. After that terrible night, we ended up staying with the Regout family for over three years.

The next morning their son Jean Claude, who still lived at home, offered to go back to Aunt Milette's and retrieve our suitcases. He was a lawyer, but he didn't practice law. Instead, he owned a chain of Sinclair gas stations throughout the region. When he returned with our bags, Jean Claude remarked that Aunt Milette had thrown our belongings into the street in a huff, insulted that a total stranger had come to claim them. We never saw her again.

Madame Regout, as I came to call her, had a beautiful three-story home filled with sculptures and antiques. Several cats lounged lazily on the landings, hissing in great annoyance whenever I walked by. A dissonant parade of twelve or more felines inside this otherwise immaculate home darted in and out of rooms and stalked me with watchful green eyes from behind the sculptures.

It was very dark inside, but all the homes in Brussels seemed cast in gray, and we soon grew accustomed to the gloomy, rainy weather. My room was on the top floor next to Jean Claude's, and Mama's was on the second floor. Though I was an older teenager now, Mama and I had slept in the same bed for most of my life. We had learned to make even the skinniest mattresses fit both of us, carefully positioning my feet near her head, her legs wedged near my ears. Another trick was "spooning" each other side-by-side, which we called "the chair" position because it was like sitting in my mother's lap in a chair. Now we not only had separate beds, but separate rooms on different floors as well.

Madame Regout was a petite woman who suffered from lymphedema, an accumulation of fluid in her legs. Sometimes her legs would become so swollen that she could hardly walk, and when she climbed the stairs she would have to rest between floors on the benches that decorated the landings. More than once, I saw the lip of her leather pumps cutting deeply into her ankles, but she rarely complained.

Their numerous grandchildren often frequented the Regout home, running up and down the stairwells, their shouts of laughter filling the halls. I was happy to help take care of them during their visits, and Mama helped around the house, too. However, my mother did not want me being a nanny for the rest of my life. She wanted me to go to school even though we clearly did not have the money for me to do so in Brussels. Another obstacle was that every school taught in French, and I knew very little French.

I took some French classes when I was younger, but I was hardly conversational. I could point and say "door" in French, but my limited vocabulary would not help me take notes in class. After talking with the Regouts about my interest in medicine, Madame Regout suggested I attend a private Catholic nursing school on the outskirts of the city, ten minutes by tram. She just happened to know the director, who would get me in right away despite my embarrassingly limited language skills.

St. Ignace, 84 Avenue de la Faisendrie, was less of a nurse training school like those in the United States and more of a preparatory school for wealthy girls. On Monday, chauffeurs lined the front entrance, dropping off the girls for their poetry and literature classes. At the end of the week, the girls would return to their parents' beautiful homes, and I would return to Madame Regout's for the weekend to care for the grand-children. I never let on at school that I was their nanny. The Regouts' driver would be in line with all the other chauffeurs at the end of the week, waiting for me, so no one thought I was any different from them.

When we first moved to the Regouts, we ate alongside them for meals in their family dining room. The Regouts, very status-conscious members of society in Brussels, soon deter-mined that we were no longer overnight guests, and yet we were nothing like their other wealthy, well-bred family mem-bers and friends. Over time, we moved to the kitchen to eat our meals with the driver and cleaning lady, and everyone felt more comfortable.

Mama worried about me staying upstairs next to Jean Claude's room. I tried to tell her not to worry; we both knew he was a little eccentric and reclusive. I reminded her how I'd caught him talking to one of the cats, Puss Puss, in Eng-lish on more than one occasion. She remained unconvinced. Being the protective mother that she was, she sensed that af-ter a while we might wear out our welcome at the Regouts. Although they were generous, Mama feared Madame Regout might somehow drive a wedge between us. She wanted us to become more independent and not rely on them so much for what we needed. And so Mama began a determined search for an alternate living arrangement.

Abbé Guy de Ryckel was a young, wealthy Catholic priest who served at nearby St. Michel Church and also helped ar-range for my education. The Regouts had graciously offered to pay for half of my tuition. This Catholic church covered the other half. My mother explained our situation to Abbé Guy, and he offered to let her live in a small apartment above the church in exchange for helping him. She served as his receptionist and housekeeper, answering the phone and typing his sermons. He thought of her as his mother and me his "little sister," which he often called me.

However, her efforts to provide another place for me to stay with her on weekends did not go as she intended. When I left my dorm room at St. Ignace for the weekend, I sometimes stayed with her, but the Regouts needed me more often than not. My mother grew increasingly despondent over the distance between us and more convinced that the Regouts had other plans in mind for me that involved their son, Jean Claude, and not necessarily my education.

SEEDS

CHAPTER SIX

ROOTS

M ADAME REGOUT WAS LOVELY AND ELEGANT. I RARELY saw Monsieur Regout, and he died a year after we arrived. Unlike Mama, I rather enjoyed being in their home and pretending I was one of the girls at school who went home to their wealthy estates on the weekends. I felt none of my mother's threatening feelings of inferiority. On the contrary, I looked to the Regout household for stability.

When we arrived in Belgium in 1968, I was seventeen and I cherished having my own room at the Regouts' house—and my own dorm room at St. Ignace. In some ways, I preferred my dorm room because it was entirely my own and I could decorate it any way that I wished. I kept the same room during all four of my years there and covered the walls with photos of my new friends and pictures I cut from magazines. I was also obsessed with my bed. It was metal-framed and very small, with a wooden shelf fixed above that ran the length of the bed, for holding knick-knacks. I took several photos of me just sitting there proudly. To me, my room seemed luxurious because I didn't have to share it with anyone. I even had my own sink, and I felt extremely pampered and entirely indulgent.

The first few weeks I was there, I would lie in bed each night and think to myself, *This is so good. This is so, so good.* I could hear the shrill of girls' voices as they talked and flirted with their boyfriends on the hall phone just outside my room, but to me all was still and silent behind my door. Here, inside a room of my own, I felt safe.

I started developing hobbies and interests, including sculpting. My mother was a painter, but I never took to it because she criticized my first few attempts to paint. At the nursing school, we were required to serve different rotations at various hospitals in order to observe. One semester, I did a rotation at a mental institute named La Ramé, where I helped calm the patients with art therapy. Here I had the opportunity to make belts, jewelry and other crafts, including sculpting. La Ramé was where I developed a love for sculpting, something I still enjoy doing today in the small studio inside my home.

I was the new girl on campus at St. Ignace, constantly mispronouncing my words in French and sending the other girls at school into peals of laughter. Instead of making fun of me, they actually liked me and thought it was cute the way I confused words like heure (hour) and beurre (butter). I remember sitting in my dorm room in the evenings with several new friends scattered around, urging me to pronounce a new phrase or two in French for their amusement.

"Say something…anything!" they would prod.

Eager to please, I would sound it out and they would all collapse together in laughter at how ridiculous I sounded. Even though I smiled with them, I knew that the novelty would wear off quickly. I did not want to mispronounce words years later, when people would expect me to know the language properly. So I studied hard and learned French very quickly, thanks in part to my mother, who was fluent. I made my friends correct me after each mistake, and I would repeat the proper pronunciation of each word or phrase silently for hours afterward.

They came up with a nickname for me, *petit chou*, which

means "little cabbage," though I don't know exactly why they named me that! It was better than "Poopie," I decided, and I soaked up their attention like a sponge.

For the first time in my life, I had friends. We watched television in the day room or sunbathed in the courtyard in our swimsuits. We listened to Simon and Garfunkel on a little transistor radio I had in my room and sang along with the Beatles. Mama never let me listen to this music at home with her—she was far too classy for popular music. Sometimes the nuns took us on weekend retreats to nearby villages, where we did crafts with leather and painted ceramics. I also received a little camera as a gift, and I carried it with me most of the time. Before long I became the unofficial photographer in the group, snapping hundreds of photos—most likely because I knew a girl who worked in a nearby photo lab.

Dominique and Jacqueline were my closest friends. One time Jacqueline invited me on a trip to the Flemish coast for the weekend. I didn't tell my mother I was going; she thought I had gone to Madame Regout's as usual. Jacqueline and I played on the beach and stayed in a cheap motel where they charged extra to change the sheets! We thought that was absurd to pay money to get fresh sheets, so we just stripped off the dirty ones and slept on the mattress.

Jacqueline also had a moped on campus. We rode together to St. Michel Hospital for our hospital rotations and often managed to sneak out through a dorm window after hours to grab *pommes de frites* (French fries) in town. They were delicious, served in a rolled cone of waxed paper with a dollop of mayonnaise to dip the fries in. It's a wonder that we were never caught, since the tempting smell of salty, fried potatoes lingered on our clothes and in the halls for hours after our return.

When we didn't ride the moped to the hospital, we waited outside the school to hitch a ride to the hospital for our rotations. It was the 1960s, and young people often hitchhiked around town and throughout Europe. Workers would pull up to the sidewalk, pick up several girls and drop them off at the hospital on their way to work. Otherwise, it was twenty minutes by tram. The girls took secret pleasure in indiscriminately hopping in cars with strangers in the middle of Brussels, knowing their aristocratic parents would have been horrified. In contrast, I had lived with strangers most of my life, so hitching a ride to work with them didn't seem as daring. But I didn't tell anyone that. I made sure I giggled gleefully in our mischief just like all of the other girls. They never asked me questions about my background or my father. They simply assumed my life was similar to their own, since I went to the same school and lived with the wealthy and well-known Regouts.

Once a friend of mine, Monique, invited me to a soirée. She came from an extremely wealthy, noble family. Of course, I had nothing to wear to this high-society occasion. I eagerly accepted her invitation and secretly went to work on my first attempt at sewing a dress.

"How hard could it be?" I asked myself. I bought several yards of the most expensive material a few francs could afford and spread it out on the floor of my dorm room. Lying down on top of it, I carefully cut a jagged "A-line" pattern along the outline of my body.

I never measured a single cut. In my country, the tailors didn't read or write, so they never used written measurements. Instead, they used a string to measure various lengths and tied various knots where their cuts should be. I assumed I could do just as well and proceeded to sew and cut the material by instinct instead of using a pattern. Let's just say I'm a much better doctor than I am a seamstress.

I carefully hemmed the sleeves, which to my dismay ended up very uneven. I looked in the mirror and hoped a well-placed rubber band on the longer sleeve, plus some strategically brushed strands of my long hair, could fix it.

Monique arranged for a driver to pick me up and take me to her chateau. I nervously did some last minute pulling at several loose strings on my hem in the car on the way there. Long before we pulled up to the home, I could hear the lovely quartet music flowing out of the leaded glass doorway and saw ladies dressed in exquisite, beaded formals gracefully walking arm-in-arm with their tuxedo-clad escorts across the drive. Monique's home was a gray and white French chateau with hundreds of rooms and ornately landscaped grounds. It was like being on a movie set, golden light glowing from every window.

I was shaking inside, but summoned every bit of self-confidence I had to walk up the few steps to the door and give the doormen my name. My mouth was so dry, my voice sounded like a mouse squeak. The two men exchanged haughty glances at me standing before them in my homemade dress.

They asked me to repeat my name, which I did.

They halfheartedly scanned the guest list that one of them held and promptly informed me I was not on the list and could not come in. By that point, I felt as though every eye was on me. I felt hot tears beginning to sting my eyes, so I just turned around without a word and went back to the waiting car.

"Take me back to the school," I told the driver, not making eye contact. I did not want him to see me crying.

On Monday, Monique found me in class and came up to me with a worried expression on her face. "Where were you?"

she asked, grabbing my hands in hers and plopping into the desk next to me. "I looked and looked for you, but you never came."

"They wouldn't let me in, Monique," I whispered to her.

At that, her face fell. In a moment, she understood.

I'd never told my friends that my mother was a cleaning lady living in an apartment full of donated furniture above a church. Or that I slept in the same bed with her whenever I visited her. When I went to Mama's, I always had the driver drop me off first in front of Madame Regout's. Without going inside, I would wait until his car rounded the corner and then walk a few blocks to the tram that would take me to Mama's.

I told the other girls in my dorm enough facts and left out enough other details to let them believe my mother was an office receptionist. I even took a picture of her sitting behind the priest's desk and one more of her next to the church piano, though she never played a note in her life. I staged these photos in frames around my dorm room, which was exactly how my entire life felt at the time: staged.

* * *

AFTER THE experience with Monique's soirée, I learned that life had not really changed that much since my younger days on the playground in Yugoslavia, where kids had teased and taunted me for being different. I was reminded once again that I had to know my place. It was clear I would never be part of this world, although I'd made several friends and many acquaintances at school. I could pretend all I wanted that Madame Regout was my adopted family, but reality reminded me that I would never fit in their world—or anyone else's at school.

ROOTS

The people closest to my social ranking were a few girls of Flemish descent, Dutch-speaking families who represented more of the working class. I don't know how they got into an exclusive school like St. Ignace, but their token presence reminded me of the distinctions between social classes in Europe. Even though I fit better with these girls, I was not Flemish and I didn't speak Dutch. The French-speaking Valons like Monique were considered the more noble class, and they were intimidating to the other girls. Many of the Flemish girls would actually use some of the limited medical training we received and work as nurses some day. But my baroness classmates would never work a day in their lives. They were not supposed to work.

I was stuck in the middle, because I did not consider myself less than someone like Monique but I still didn't quite fit into the working class category either. Several Flemish girls invited me to their homes for the weekend many times. But I never went. I wasn't curious about their lives; I knew what it was like. I was drawn to Monique's world—what I couldn't have and had never experienced. I wanted to go there because I couldn't go there.

My Valon friends would return from weekends at home telling about their fanciful soirées and English riding lessons. I sensed they tried to downplay the details in my presence in order to avoid hurting my feelings, which made me feel even worse.

I desperately desired to blend in. To lose my accent. To speak perfect French. Ironically, I had felt that I *was* "in" with someone like Monique until I arrived at her doorstep that night. As nice to me as they were, the girls in my school would have had to peel off too many protective layers designed to keep people like me out. They could never completely weave me into their world. They had to behave by the rules, which were not necessarily of their making. They were the ironclad expectations handed down to them by their parents, as the generation before had done for them. Monique never forgave her parents for what happened that night at her house, but she was helpless to change it. I did not expect that finally making friends at school would come at such a painful price, but it was better to continue balancing precariously between the two classes in my own way rather than to be lonely again.

Another niche I found was at La Maison International, the international house for foreign students. I became their treasurer and then the president. There was a student named Franco who was visiting from Italy. He was charming and paid attention to me, although not in a romantic sense. When I introduced Mama to him, she fell in love with him. She refused to listen when I told her he did not have feelings for me other than those of friendship.

"Sasha, he is *perfect* for you," she insisted, which she knew would get to me. If Mama approved of someone, I saw them with different eyes. To please her, I wanted to like him as much as she did, but he was already engaged to another girl named Franca. With Mama's words ringing in my ear, I secretly held on to the off chance that he might leave his fiancé for me, although I didn't really want that to happen at all. But it was not meant to be.

I went out dancing a few times with my friend Dominique's brother, Charles, although that could hardly be called a romance either. I was twenty-one when I graduated, but I was more like a young teen in regards to the opposite sex, too immature to understand how relationships between guys and girls were supposed to work.

ROOTS

I once stayed for six weeks with Dominique and her family in Trieste, Italy, on vacation in their villa. I had never been on a vacation. Her stepfather was the manager of a glass factory in Trieste. Because of layoffs, his workers went on strike a few days before I arrived. The disgruntled workers threatened to kill Dominique's stepfather, so whenever we went into town, he made sure that bodyguards accompanied us. I thought it was very exciting and didn't give a thought to the danger we might have been in.

We went dancing at clubs, and Dominique and I even made a short shopping trip to Venice, where she bought me a purse. It was a leather bag with a small clutch wallet inside that had a mirror. I had never owned anything so precious. I carried it to my first opera with Dominique and kept opening and closing the clutch to peek in the mirror at myself. I was as giddy as a child. In many ways, the four years I spent in the nursing school were a delayed childhood experience for me.

Sometimes I wouldn't go visit Mama on the weekends, even when the Regouts didn't need me. I would make up some excuse that I had to stay in the dorm or that the Regouts' grandchildren were in town, but I would try to see her the next weekend.

* * *

THE SHALLOW, stunted roots of my existence were now working their way through the rich soil of these new experiences. Although each day brought a little bit of adventure my way, very little in terms of my weekly schedule changed. The predictability of a class schedule, lights out in the dorm every night and even three regular meals a day in the cafeteria were a balm to the fractured existence that had been my life up to that point.

I found my routine comforting: going home on weekends and returning on Monday to the same dorm room, with all my things in place, exactly how I had left them. The same people were there in class every day and they recognized me. I didn't have to worry where I would sleep the next night. I didn't have to worry about my next meal.

I could even predict with certainty the cafeteria menu every Friday: they called it *American filet* (it was actually steak tar tar with capers), French fries and chocolate mousse. The repetition and predictability drove my other friends crazy, and they loudly complained about the deprivation of it all. While they would moan about the overly protective nuns watching over their shoulders, I often felt guilty because I actually took comfort in making curfew.

Before our time in Belgium, Mama and I had learned to befriend the one thing that we could count on—change. Change had become the norm; constant flux was our ironic source of stability. Initially, learning to live amid the predictability that accompanied our lives in Brussels took some getting used to. Culturally speaking, there is very little change throughout the entire country of Belgium. In general, people in Belgium keep the same jobs throughout their lives. Twenty years after I left Brussels and moved to America, I went back to the hospital where I had made my rotations as a student at St. Ignace and saw the same people in the same clerical positions they were in twenty years ago. Many lived in the same homes for their entire lives, family homes that had been passed down through the generations.

When I lived there, I found this cultural element of "sameness" comforting. I felt secure and anchored; there was a part of me that never wanted my time in Belgium to end. However, no matter how well things were going, the fear that it would all be taken from me unexpectedly never went away. The thought haunted me and I told myself I should not enjoy it too much or I would risk being disappointed.

I wanted so much to share with Mama all that was happening in my new life at school, but I hesitated. The very things that thrilled me seemed to terrify her. Although I intentionally withheld information from her about my whereabouts and schedule at school, she still knew I was growing more independent of her.

Whenever I went to visit Mama, the twinkling stars of excitement that dotted my life now faded into the stark daylight of her reality. My mother was a cleaning lady. That was how she saw herself. Partway during my schooling, she started taking on other jobs to pay part of my tuition herself—her attempt to distance me even more from the Regouts. She worked for an appliance store, dusting the stovetops and sweeping the sidewalks outside in front of the store.

"I cleaned the streets of Brussels," she would often wistfully recall after we moved to America. Inside I would roll my eyes, wondering once more why she had to be so dramatic. She had a flair for embellishment, but she was telling the truth. She did clean the streets, as did many displaced people from Yugoslavia and other countries at that time. Sometimes, for a special treat, my mother and I would eat at a Yugoslavian restaurant in Brussels. There, we met brilliant former Yugoslav engineers who were now dishwashers. Just as often, we saw Yugoslav doctors who were now hotel doormen. After dinner at the restaurant, they would sit around in groups, smoking and drinking Slivovitz (a strong plum brandy) and Turkish coffee, trading melancholy memories about a potpourri of things they missed. Included in this list was the incomparable taste of one-day-old cheese—a treat they swore one could only get in Yugoslavia. These political refugees were all free now—free to crack jokes about Tito's regime and speak as they pleased, but that was about it. They were not free to be who they really were or to make a significant contribution to society.

Even when she was a young woman in prison, Mama used her education. She was forced to work as an accountant for the regime from her prison cell. The Communists said to the ex-doctors, ex-lawyers and ex-engineers who were now their captives, "This is not a hotel. We're feeding you. You're sleeping here. You need to work."

The idea of prisoners sitting around, lifting weights and eating free meals as we often see in America would have been ludicrous in Yugoslavia. However, even though she was now free in Belgium, she was unable to move up to a position equal to her training. Her PhD was useless there.

She knew she would never have the social standing that her sister Koka or her mother Sida had, nor did she necessarily want it. But she did want a basic level of respect. I remember when we first came to America and a young man she worked with called her by her first name, Katarina, instead of Ms. Maksimovich. I understood we were now in a different culture and a different time, but she winced at his casual tone and I saw the pain in her tired eyes. Katarina Maksimovich had become a nobody, not even worth a young man's respect for his elder.

CHAPTER SEVEN

COMING TO AMERICA

IN SEPTEMBER OF 1972, WE WERE STILL LIVING IN BELGIUM, and the process for our immigration to America was coming to an end after three years of filing papers and completing forms. Although we were offered Belgium citizenship, we declined because we wanted to become Americans. For the four years that we lived in Brussels, we had no citizenship in any country. Typed on our paperwork was the ominous-sounding word: "stateless."

Instead of feeling sorry for us, my mother was very proud of that designation and carried the piece of paper with her everywhere. Whenever anyone in Belgium asked for ID, she gladly showed them. She didn't want to be Belgian—and who knows if they really wanted to take her on either! In her opinion, Belgium was a closed society, very guarded about those they let in to their ranks. Saying she didn't want to be part of them was her way of countering their arrogance.

Caritas Catolica was a charitable Catholic organization that was responsible for sponsoring our immigration to America. Their officials wrote a letter of guarantee, agreeing to pay for our expenses in America until we found jobs. Usually family members already living in the States would be the responsible party, but we knew no one. My mother didn't even tell her mother or sister when we left, but they had not spoken in years anyway. When all of our immigration paperwork was in motion, it became a waiting game.

Six months earlier, in January that same year, while we were still filing immigration forms, I received some unexpected news. I was with my mother one afternoon when the phone rang at the church office. Abbé knocked on my mother's door and told me I had a phone call. He knew it had to be for us because the man on the other end of the line did not speak French. Mama and I exchanged nervous glances, and without saying a word, we both realized what the call was about. I went downstairs to the phone and recognized the voice of my brother, Petar. He told me our father had died earlier that day.

I had always resented my father for leaving us. Now, he had left for good; and yet instead of feeling rage, I felt a deep sadness—most of which centered on my mother's reaction to his death. I didn't realize until the moment I told her the news how much she loved him. Outside of the three-day relationship with Nino that turned out to be a disaster, my mother had never married. Never loved anyone else. And never felt another man's love. My father was her only one.

His death closed a significant chapter in my life—just as I was starting a new one he would never get to read. Little did I know that this pattern of closing and opening, death and new life, would repeat itself again thirteen short years later.

* * *

EVERYONE FROM ST. IGNACE went their separate ways the summer I graduated from nursing school. I never expected it would be the last time I saw most of my new friends. I did not know I would soon leave for America. That summer I volunteered as a counselor at a Catholic camp for children. I had my diploma, but I was not yet a practicing nurse. Still, I was the best at taking out splinters. A competition arose among the children to see who had the biggest splinter. The campers would come to me holding their wounded finger in the air for all to see and I would seat them beside me, removing the offending splinters in order of size, biggest to smallest. One freckle-faced little girl was playing a game and slid on her backside on the wooden porch, which resulted in a splinter in her left cheek the size of a pencil! Her name went to the top of the splinter ranking board outside my station, which these Catholic kids jokingly called "the place of suffering," and remained unchallenged. I worked there all summer and returned home in August, just a few weeks before we found out we would be leaving for America.

Whenever I told people my mother and I were trying to immigrate to America, many scoffed at the idea. "Why would you want to go *there*?" they asked, as if the word left a bad taste in their mouths. Their perception of Americans was that they were rude, loud and unrefined, unlike proper and dignified Belgians. Nevertheless, my mother was intrigued with America.

She was always talking to people in Yugoslav restaurants in Brussels about what America would be like. Everyone in the working class seemed to have relatives in one country or another, and it was easy to become enamored with life on the other side of the world. We didn't necessarily know one country from another, as far as which one would be the best place to live, but America kept coming to our minds.

No doubt, some of my mother's fascination with America came from the movies she'd seen or the books she'd read. I knew some English words like "cowboy," "dollar" and "I love you," but outside of the few exaggerated images we'd created in our mind of what life in America would be like, we didn't really know what to expect. All my mother knew was that America was a place where you could talk and share your opinions. And she had many opinions.

We weren't necessarily drawn to the so-called American dream of owning a nice car and living in a lovely home, like some might presume. Material possessions and the opportunity for success that America could afford did not lure us, even though we owned very little when we left Belgium. Once again we brought nothing with us other than what we could fit into our suitcases.

For my mother, the dream was solely about being free. Freedom is a broad image and means different things to different people. I've sometimes thought that my mother's idea of freedom could have been fulfilled nearly anywhere, because she just wanted to be free to express herself. She was a cleaning lady among people who had no concept of or interest in talking about ideas. Communicating to people who didn't really care about life's bigger issues and the beauty of the mind did nothing to satisfy her needs. Her "peers" were uneducated cleaning ladies, mechanics and restaurant owners. Most were there in Belgium for financial reasons alone, economic refugees just looking for a place to live and earn money. One could name both my mother and a dishwasher "refugees," but there was a world of difference between them. The refugees who held all their possessions in a bag tied with a rope were the ones desperate to escape, as we had been years earlier. However, enough time had passed since those early days. We no longer felt destitute. We weren't on the streets. We were prepared to go to America on a plane, wearing our best dresses and our black patent shoes.

Our immigration paperwork came through in late August. The letter from Caritas Catolica had been approved; by September we were gone. I wrote a few hurried letters to friends like Dominique and Jacqueline, but other than a rushed good-bye with the Regouts, we left much the same way we'd left anywhere else we'd ever lived. Mother did not own any of the furniture in her church apartment, and we were able to pack only a few well-worn suitcases to take with us. We closed the door and never looked back.

We left Brussels on September 18, 1972 on our way to Cologne, Germany to catch our trans-Atlantic flight to America. Early on, we were told we could go to Sacramento or New York City. For the first time in our lives, we had a choice. Fortunately, that one came easy. We'd never heard of a place called Sacramento, so we chose New York by default.

* * *

WE ARRIVED IN New York at four in the morning on September 20. I remember the date since it was my mother's birthday. An unusual thing happened because we had started all our paperwork before we even arrived in the U.S. We received our green cards the day we set foot in New York—a process that usually takes years. We were thrilled how things seemed to be going our way right from the start.

Mama had been saying for years that when she finally arrived in America she would "kiss the ground beneath her." She'd likely seen this enacted in a movie and thought it would be a fitting tribute to do so herself. At four in the morning inside the Kennedy airport, she looked around at the filthy tile floors littered with debris and announced, "Oh well, I'll kiss my new country another time." We laughed and kept walking.

As I walked through the airport, I stared at the exaggerated height of people in platform shoes and their bell-bottom pants. In my country, I had never seen an African American up close, and a tall, black security guard was standing near the luggage carousel watching me. He looked stiff as a statue, almost lifeless, but his eyes were warm and dark. I marveled at how his hair glistened all over with a clear gel, his hat sitting neatly on top of his seventies-style afro.

We saw our bags tumble onto the conveyor belt and make their way around toward us, but when we tried to pick up the over-stuffed suitcases by their handles, the black fake-leather cardboard sides burst and spilled the contents everywhere. Several of my mother's canvases were rolled up in tubes inside our bags, along with several pieces of wood and cardboard she'd painted when paper became too expensive and a variety of oil brushes. Pieces of our lives were scattered all over the conveyor belt like bits of shattered glass. I was desperate, but neither of us spoke enough English to ask someone to help us.

I had a little American tourist book with me, and I hurriedly flipped through the pages, stopping on a drawing of a man on the side of the road with the hood up on his car. The word, "Help" was typed underneath the picture. Holding my place with my finger, I took the book with me to the black security guard around the corner. I pointed to the picture of the man and sounded out the word, "Help." I motioned toward the luggage carousel, but he just stared at me, not understanding what I meant.

Suddenly, he put his finger in the air, signaling for me to wait a minute. He walked away, so I thought he just didn't understand me. I went back to the suitcases and resumed putting our clothes and belongings back inside. However, the hinges were broken and it was like trying to get toothpaste back into the tube.

Much to our surprise and relief, the guard returned a few minutes later with rope. He carefully helped us put our things back inside, tied the suitcases closed and walked us to the Caritas bus. He was very nurturing and caring. This was my first experience with an American, and I knew in an instant that all the preconceptions I'd heard about Americans being uncaring and rude were untrue. We felt more at home in this stranger's presence than we'd felt with the people we lived among for years in Belgium.

My mother and I were the only women on the bus, surrounded by other immigrants sponsored by Caritas. No one spoke, but that was okay because we couldn't understand each other anyway. My first impression of America as we looked out the windows was that everything was bigger: the stores, the people, the cars. I kept blinking, trying to adjust my eyes to the elongated buildings and skyscrapers.

Our destination was the Wolcott hotel in Manhattan. When we got to the hotel, it was still early morning, but several ladies stood around out in front and warmly greeted the men as we shuffled past them. Once we were in our room, I recall thinking that for such a big city, where buildings created shadows all day long on the streets below, they sure made little beds.

We did not realize at the time that people could rent a room at the Wolcott for an hour at a time—or ten minutes if they desired. The hotel featured community bathrooms at the ends of the halls, so we began to recognize certain people. I was impressed at how the ladies staying at the hotel were all beautiful with lots of makeup—and so friendly. They tried teaching me a few English words and were warm toward everyone, especially the men. I had no idea they were prostitutes. They were such hard workers, but I was curious why I never saw them in the mornings. I just assumed they all worked somewhere during the day because I saw them out in the halls every evening. These ladies of the night became my first friends in America.

* * *

EVERY DAY I had to learn something to survive in this strange new country. Our sponsors, Caritas Catolica, paid us $2.50 per day while we looked for work. I held my first fistful of U.S. coins in my hand and tried to sort through which ones were worth what. No one could explain to my satisfaction why a nickel, which was bigger than a dime, was actually worth less money. Once, I got into an argument with a man selling sandwiches because he took more of my nickels ("big change") than dimes ("little change"). I just assumed he was cheating me.

I had also bought some English language tapes before leaving Brussels to get a head start on learning to speak English. I listened to the lessons faithfully, tuning my ear to the inflections and tones repeated in the little stories they told. One day in downtown Manhattan, it dawned on me that no one was asking me anything that drew on my lessons. The story of Rip Van Winkle never came up in everyday conversation; nor did anyone ask me about Mr. Jones in the garden with his dog. I decided I needed more pragmatic lessons if I were going to get along in this country, so I soon turned to the television.

My mother and I watched TV in our hotel room, but we didn't watch it the way Americans did. We were more interested in the commercials than the television shows. We liked that the same commercials repeated over and over again, helping us pick up on certain phrases. We also discovered that we could hear them even if we left the room because the volume would go up whenever a commercial came on. If we were in the next room and heard one of our favorite commercials, we would dash back in to practice it. Mama's first sentence in English was, "My Toyota is fantastic!" We didn't have a car, but she was very convincing whenever she said it.

My favorites were, "Smell clean with Lifebuoy" and re-enacting Pat Boone's old commercial where he bites into a cracker and says, "Mmmm, good cracker." We tried to generalize these fragments of English, so I would eat a piece of bread and say, "Mmmm, good cracker." For the first few months in America, Mama and I lived in the hotel room and talked to each other "in commercials."

Although I liked the friends I made at the Wolcott Hotel, we wanted to move away from there and into a nicer place as soon as possible. During the first night there, we fell into the small, metal-framed bed and turned off the light—our head and feet at opposite ends like usual. I woke up a few minutes later feeling something crawling up my leg. I flipped on the light just in time to see half a dozen giant roaches scatter across the sheets and hide in the dark under the bed. To keep the roaches away, we slept with the lights on every night thereafter. We laid socks across our eyes and pretended we were first-class passengers on a luxury plane wearing our eye masks.

Every day, we checked the job board at the Caritas main office. I interviewed for a nurse's aide job at Royal Hospital in the Bronx. I had worked my entire life, but I'd never had a job with set hours and a paycheck. For the first time ever, I hoped to support my mother with my wages.

Royal was a private Jewish hospital. The director's wife

was French and she loved me because I spoke French. He thought it would be cute to have a French-speaking nurse around the hospital, so he agreed to hire me as a nurse's aide working under the supervision of a nurse from Yugoslavia who was a Gypsy.

Unlike the director, the patients were not as charmed that I only spoke French. People were sick and needed my attention, but I could not understand a word they said. Every day it was the same. Both the patient and I would go through elaborate pantomimes, pointing at various objects and body parts, mouthing out words. But it was no use. Only after a patient wet the bed did I finally understand what he was desperately trying to tell me.

I was in no way ready to be a nurse in a new country. I didn't understand the system of measurement, and I couldn't even take a temperature. I took an English nursing test, which I promptly failed. The Gypsy charge nurse and another nurse, an Indian man, helped me study and the second time I took the test I passed. I became a medication nurse, preparing and delivering scheduled medication twice a day.

By this time, we had moved out of the hotel in Manhattan and into a small apartment in the Bronx. The beds had itchy wool blankets, so one day we decided to purchase some sheets at a small neighborhood store. In Yugoslavia, there weren't many choices when it came to bed linens and towels. Everything came in one color: white. As I walked, I pictured the white sheets I wanted and practiced what to say to the sales clerk.

When I walked into the store, I saw a buxom black woman with enormous cleavage sitting behind the cash register. Her fingers boasted several cheap gold rings and she was busy filing her nails.

My mother, Katarina Maksimovich (middle) with her younger sister, Koka, and their mother, Sida, 1935. The sisters were as different on the inside as they were on the outside.

Outside Boris and Sida's home in Belgrade (my grandparents). My mother is holding the doll. Their house was rumored to have become one of Tito's summer homes.

My grandfather Boris was murdered. A young and promising judge, his elaborate funeral was the first and only time they used white for mourning instead of black.

Nestorovich, my mother and Sida. My mother loved accompanying Nestorovich on his travels—he always wore a starched, white scarf because of a wound on his neck.

My great-grandfather and namesake, Svetislav Stanich, photographed one week before I was born. He loved and cared for my mother as his own child.

One of the only photos I have of my father, Ivan Vukelja. He was a captain in the military.

As a child, dressed in my usual tomboy attire with cropped hair.

My first dress and a doll borrowed from the photographer. I was staying with "relatives" who made me look like a girl for the first time!

Chako, one of the only bright spots of my childhood—in my memory, he is always smiling. A man who looks as though he wouldn't hurt a bird.

After the 1963 earthquake in Skopje, Macedonia. My home and school were destroyed, but Mama and I were happy to be alive. What remains of the train station is in the background.

One of the only photos I have of Mama and me together, smiling. We were so proud of our matching raincoats.

I discovered I had a teenaged brother, Petar, (whose father was Ivan). We began a secret correspondence.

My Jesuit brothers. Father Cobi (left), seated next to the woman whose apartment we shared. Father Svoljshak is on the far right.

Saint John Maximovich. Mama was so proud of this "holy man" in our family tree—she framed this postcard photo of him.

With Madame Regout in Brussels, Belgium. I will always be grateful to her.

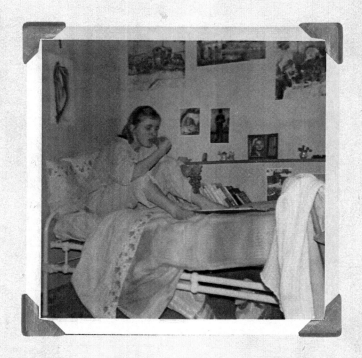

In my dorm room at St. Ignace—I have dozens of photos of me on my bed.

The infamous homemade dress worn to a high-society soirée. I did not get in the door.

I made my mother pose at the piano to impress my friends. She never played.

Purchasing my first car and getting my American driver's license on the same day! Standing next to the Audi Fox.

On the way to buy another car. My life's savings is in the yellow plastic bag...I was mistaken for the cleaning lady inside the dealership.

Outside the officer's quarters in my Public Health uniform.

In my second year of medical school, I changed services and joined the Army. I am on a field training exercise in this photo.

Mama at my graduation from medical school. She is wearing the dress I later chose for her funeral. My friend, Antonia, on the left.

A typical day at one of the clinics in Africa. The man in the foreground has leprosy—note the missing fingers on his left hand.

My friend and patient, General Bill Schneider, gave me away at my wedding, 1991.

Maxi with Larry at two years old.

Saying goodbye to Boris (holding Simba tightly) on his first visit to Tyler. It would be six months before we could see our son again, this time in Russia.

Grandpa Ward, the grandfather I never had. I love him dearly.

Race for the Cure participants. I made the t-shirts that say, "Live! Live! Don't just exist!" Maxi is standing with me on the front row. My friend, Freda, is the fourth from the right, back row.

Coming from the hospital to celebrate at the finish line with one of my patients. Race for the Cure, 2008.

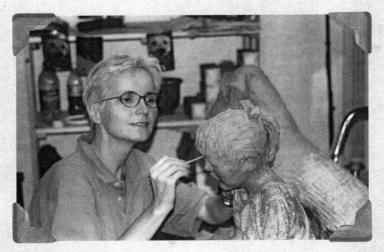

My sculpting is therapy for me.

I'm so blessed to have my family: Larry, Maxi and Boris (2009).

"Hello," I greeted her and smiled confidently, choosing my words deliberately. "I would like a big, long, white shit for the bed," I said. I was so proud, giving her all of the information in English.

The lady dropped her nail file on the counter. "You want what, honey?"

I decided to slow down and enunciate. "Do... you... have... any... long, white shits for the bed?"

She started laughing and her cleavage was shaking like jelly in a jar. Her laugh was so jovial and kind that I smiled, too. But what was so funny?

"You want a white one, huh? How long do you want this shit?" she managed to say, her breasts still heaving.

Now I was truly puzzled. What kind of question was that? Of course, I wanted a white one. Was there any other kind? I wasn't sure of the length of the bed, so I held my arms out wide. "About this long?" I suggested.

"Delmar, come here," she called to a man working in the back of the store. "Help this lady find what she needs." A black man wearing a patchwork shirt and platform shoes suddenly surfaced from the multi-colored curtain of beads hanging over the doorway.

"Go on," she urged me, trying hard not to crack up again. "Tell him what you want."

"I want a long white shit for the bed," I repeated for Delmar.

I was convinced by now that I was somehow saying the most ignorant thing possible. Delmar muffled his laugh, but the woman was already on her feet and making her way around the counter to me. She put her arm around my shoulders and said, "Honey, what you want is a *sheet*." She drew out her "eee" for effect. "You have to stretch it. Now you try."

I nodded and repeated, "Sheeeeeeet. Sheeeeeeeet." I didn't know where to stop the stretching, so I held the word as long as I could and searched her face for clues. She held up her arm and gave a karate chop through the air. "That's enough."

"Now, we got all kinds of sheets. Pink ones. Blue ones. Paisley ones. Ones with flowers on them. Are you sure you just want white?"

Delmar and the nice woman (who I later discovered was the store owner) showed me the linens, and I picked out two sets—a daisy pillowcase, striped sheets and a solid color bottom sheet, all still in my linen closet today. When I went home, I told my mother what had happened. The woman at the store had laughed at me, but she met me halfway. We still didn't know what the "shit" was. We just knew that it had to be stretched if you wanted to say it right.

A dry cleaner was right next door to the linen store, but it turned out to be miles away from the kindness I'd found there. In Europe, it's common to pay a deposit when you drop off your clothes and pay the remainder when you return to pick them up. When I visited this dry cleaner, I assumed it worked the same way. Still new to English, I handed over my bundle of clothes and asked the man, "Do I need to leave the *opposite*?"

The word I wanted was "deposit," but I could tell by his expression that I had chosen the wrong word. As I did whenever I was unsure of a word, I threw out several pronunciations that sounded close, expecting the other person to meet me halfway. Not this man. I could see in his cold eyes that he wasn't interested in understanding what I meant.

He pushed the clothes I laid on the counter back towards me and sneered, "When you learn how to speak English, you come back." Years later, when we moved out of Manhattan to the Bronx, I did go back. One day when I was in my old neighborhood, a "going out of business" sign caught my eye in the window of the store where I'd bought my sheets. On a whim, I decided to go in and was surprised to see my buxom friend still there. "You may not remember me, but I was in your store several years ago…" I started.

"White shit!" she exclaimed and jumped to her feet, moving toward the thin white woman talking to her.

"It's an inside joke!" I assured the other stunned customers, in case they feared a racial clash might break out before their eyes. We hugged and shared a laugh together. I bought a couple of things and, as I was leaving, decided to pay a visit next door to the dry cleaner. Immediately, I recognized the man behind the counter as the same man from years ago. However, I hadn't recalled his heavy Polish accent. As I listened to him impatiently take people's orders, it was obvious that he could barely manage to bark at them with broken English.

When it was my turn at the counter, I did exactly what watching so many American television commercials had taught me. I turned the volume up so I could get everyone's attention. I cleared my throat and said to him, "I came here several years ago to have my clothes cleaned and you refused to serve me. You told me to come back when I learned English. Well, here I am!" I could tell in an instant that he knew exactly who I was, though years had passed. Still, he averted his eyes from me, pretending he didn't know what I was talking about.

I continued, "Listening to you just now, I can tell you probably came to this country from somewhere else, like I did, and didn't know English. And you *still* don't speak correct English. In fact, I'd say my English is better than yours! I came here because you asked me to and because I wanted to tell you to give everyone a chance. Just because people speak funny doesn't mean that they're stupid." The people standing around me broke into spontaneous applause and some customers even left! It felt good to keep my promise to return to that store.

* * *

INITIALLY, IT WAS difficult for my mother to find a job. We were on welfare for a few weeks. One evening I took some food stamps to the grocery store around the corner to buy some toilet paper, bread, milk and other basics.

When the cashier saw that I intended to use the stamps to pay, she began separating my paper goods from the food items. I promptly pushed them all back together in a pile on the counter. She looked at me strangely and divided them once more— and I gathered them together again. This went on for a minute or two, until she finally explained that the stamps were for food items only. I didn't have the money for the paper goods. It was awkward and I was very embarrassed. I heard a woman in line behind me say, "It's people like you who are taking away our jobs." I was crushed. I wasn't trying to take anything away from anyone. I felt like a beggar just trying to survive. I cried on my way home and never used the stamps again.

I also enrolled in Lehman College in the Bronx (part of the City University of New York system) and began using all my spare time to study. I took 18 credit hours, all in French—French literature, French poetry, French tutorial. Along with these upper-level French classes, I sat in the front row of my English 101 class. My English teacher was incredibly patient with me and opened my eyes to the world of words. She helped me pinpoint exactly what I wanted to say and gave me the skills to speak precisely.

When you don't speak a language, you have to take all kinds of detours to explain and illustrate what you mean. It takes you a whole paragraph to describe what you want when a simple phrase would do it—if you knew the phrase. When I could finally narrow down the exact words and phrases I needed to use to get people to understand me, I was ecstatic.

Communicating in precise ways became even more important to me as time passed. Today, some people think I talk rather abruptly, clipping my words. Actually, I spent years practicing being precise so I wouldn't waste anyone's time trying to understand me! I don't consider being direct such a bad thing—especially in my field, where sugarcoated words can be confusing. In order to be able to fight for my patients and form a plan of attack against cancer, I have to deliver information without layers. Some have said about me, "You may not always like what she has to say, but you know exactly where you stand."

The power of words fascinated me when I was learning English, and it still does today. I remember discovering the word *iconoclastic* and trying to manipulate conversations the rest of the day just to use it in a sentence—which is not easy to do. Of course, some words continued to elude me. For example, I went swimming at "Jones Bitch" for years. No one ever corrected me and told me it was Jones *Beach*! For years, I said things like "survival of the fetus" when I meant "survival of the fittest." I was always "kicking it in the butt" when I should have been "nipping it in the bud"!

Within a year, I was filling in at the hospital on the weekends, covering for the charge nurse. I was also tutoring students at college, earning five dollars an hour from the school. Our new apartment was palatial. It had two bedrooms, a kitchen, one bathroom that my mother and I shared and even a sunken living room. For the first time, instead of losing things and leaving them behind, we began to acquire. I bought some old frames, and we framed some of my mother's favorite paintings and hung them on the bare walls. We went to used furniture stores and bought nightstands and a little cocktail table that we hauled home to repaint with thick, mahogany-colored paint. In our collection, we also had bedroom furniture, a lone rocking chair and a television in the living room. One day when we were watching Columbo on our black-and-white Zenith television, Mama leaned back in the rocking chair and it broke.

We were horrified. We could not afford to buy furniture that could break without warning. Now that we were in America, we wanted things that would last a lifetime. Mama and I were regular shoppers in Harlem, so we returned to our favorite used furniture store to buy a matching living room set. A green and gold velvet set in the corner caught our eye. The man who was helping us was a burly black man who was clearly overweight. My mother, who had put on a few pounds herself in recent years, was explaining to him in broken English and a few gestures with her hands how we wanted this furniture to last and not to break.

Mama always thought of people like dogs—if they sense you are not afraid of them, they won't attack you. My mother knew no fear. She brazenly asked this giant of a man, who must have weighed 350 pounds, if he would please sit in each piece of the furniture.

"If it no breaks, we buy it," Mama said, pleased with her consumer finesse. Without a moment's hesitation, he proceeded to do exactly as she asked, moving from piece to piece, dropping his entire weight down into the seat, then sighing and standing up with great effort. Satisfied, we bought the green and gold furniture, and it's still in my living room today, although with new upholstery.

Our apartment in the Bronx was over a bagel shop. If we left the window open, we could smell the fresh bagels, but my mother usually kept it closed because our neighbors often smoked marijuana on the fire escape!

In the bagel shop, if you bought a dozen bagels, you got one free. My favorite tradition became buying a dozen of fresh garlic and onion bagels on my way home from work, holding the warm, brown paper sack to my chest and breathing in the aroma. By the time I got off the elevator, I had usually devoured the free one and started on another.

Bagels were a splurge, of course. As were the big tubes of toothpaste, and the occasional hamburger from McDonald's my tutoring students brought me as "payment" for tutoring them extra hours beyond what the school paid me. I told my mother I was now "the bread-maker" in the family so she wouldn't have to worry about not being able to find a job. We were still on welfare, but because of the incident with the food stamps at the grocery store, we vowed never to use them again. In fact, we returned our stamps for someone else to use.

* * *

IN OUR three years in Belgium, the seedlings had grown strong and established the beginnings of a respectable root system. With our move to New York City, we felt as if we'd been uprooted and transplanted into a much larger pot. If you know anything about container gardening, transplanting is necessary. Plants rarely stay inside the tiny pot they come in at the nursery. Instead, gardeners place them in a larger pot immediately and an even much larger one after several months' growth. Otherwise, the plant's growth is stunted. It may live in the small container for a while, but it will never reach its full potential.

If my mother and I had stayed in Belgium, we would have remained at a certain level professionally until there was room for us in the next level, meaning someone in the next higher position died or moved away. Promotion is not based on one's abilities as it is in America; it's based on the need at the time. So you can be stuck in your little container for years, still alive, but not thriving or accomplishing all that you want to do. America held much more opportunity.

My mother always thought like an American, even before she fully understood the American mentality. She deeply believed that if you have the ability and the ambition, nothing should stop you from achieving all that you want in this life. In Europe, drive alone was not enough. The conditions had to be right for personal advancement and so did the timing—and sometimes that could take decades or never happen at all.

Of course, there were risks involved in transplanting to a "bigger pot." In fact, when an established plant transplants to a new container, it will often struggle to take root at first. It droops for a while and might even look like it's dying. Some days we felt so small in our giant new surroundings that it was a struggle just to survive. This readjustment to the new soil and conditions takes patience on the part of the gardener—and restraint not to toss it out when the wilted plant initially appears more dead than alive. Given time, though, the plant will re-establish roots in its new home and, as anticipated, begin to grow twice as big.

BEAUTY AND BLOOM

O UR LANDLORD WAS A DRUNK, BUT HE WAS NICE TO my mother and gave her all kinds of leftover pieces of wood on which to paint. Old doorframes. Tabletops from old furniture. Because he had sawed with the shaky hands that result from many years of drinking, all his cuts were crooked. Nevertheless, my mother didn't seem to mind as she transformed each one into useful surfaces for painting. This time in her life marked a period of prolific painting. She painted all the time, sometimes long into the night. I would often come home late from being on call at the hospital. When I woke up the next morning, she would have completed five new paintings. Looking back, this was her comfort, a place to direct all her energies because she had not yet landed a job.

Everything changed for my mother when she finally found a job at CETA, a city employment agency that allowed people on welfare to work for their paycheck. Although she was highly intelligent, my mother had a gift for connecting with all kinds of people from any background. Her coworkers, also on welfare, were what society considered undesirable: homeless people, prostitutes, criminals, delinquents, transvestites, drug addicts and others. They were taken by the kindness my mother showed them. Her complete acceptance of their colorful lives caught me by surprise, too. She'd always been so strict with me, but she overlooked many of their offenses. She

105

had a way of gently peeling back the layers of their personalities that had been so harshly judged by society and connecting to their hearts.

It was not unusual for me to come home from work and find five or six people—folks you would not talk to if you met them on the street—all crammed around the tiny dining table we'd bought in Harlem. Hanging on to my mother's every word, they listened to her telling tales from the old country for hours. She was a natural storyteller. When I retired to my room to polish my white nursing shoes each night, I could still hear my mother, leaning back in her chair and spinning a story with a mix of German, French and broken English, gesturing and acting out parts when necessary. She had everyone laughing and crying all at the same time. This was her first American audience and she was a big hit. She genuinely loved and accepted people as they were. And they loved her back.

She would cook festive meals, make sure everyone got more than enough food on their plates and then retire to a chair in the corner to watch them eat it. "Is it good?" she would ask, getting up to hover over their shoulders and provide elaborate commentary on what everyone was eating or not eating. "Take two." "Put more on your plate." "Here, try this."

No matter how successful the meal, she would say, "Oh, but it's not so good," lamenting how her guests had returned for only three helpings instead of four. These new friends soon learned to eat each helping quickly, realizing that the more they ate and the more feedback they lavished on her, the more she would cook. She gave them several of her paintings as gifts. For many of them, this was the first time anyone had showed real concern for them.

What they didn't realize was that the feeling was mutual.

For the first time, she was stable enough in her own place in life *to be able* to care for someone else. Others had always cared for us before; now she could return the favor—in a home of our own. Being able, at last, to put down roots brought beauty into our lives and the ability to bloom like never before. We were no longer stifled and stunted in a country where we could not grow. For the first time, we knew we were finally in a place we would never leave. No matter what happened, we would stay here in America.

We were familiar with hardship, but some of Mama's new friends made our lives seem uneventful and bland in comparison. These people were troubled, with problems and pasts so complicated they would never be able to unravel them. When they talked to her about their situations, she could understand only a fraction of it—partly because of her faltering English and partly because of her narrow experience with their lifestyles. I remember one time seeing a man, a transvestite, hemming his dress on our couch to wear to a date with another man. Even so, she nurtured them all the same, without an ounce of prejudice. We didn't have any family, and in a strange way, this eclectic group of people became one for us.

* * *

IN COLLEGE, I also met people unlike anyone I'd ever met before—Puerto Ricans, African Americans—all underprivileged students who were getting their first real break. I could relate to them, and I became a very popular tutor because no one felt intimidated by me. I had an accent. I had not lived a privileged existence. They could ask me anything and I would try to help them. Although I had the paperwork from my education at St.

Ignace, Lehman enrolled me as a freshman because it took so long to translate my transcript.

I also dabbled for the first time with the American tradition of dating. A Polish woman who worked at a nearby bakery had become a friend of ours, and she insisted on setting me up. I had exactly two blind dates. I remember them because they both ended the same way, at the same time: five minutes after meeting my mother. One guy came in and sat down on our loveseat across from her. She was so proud of the green and gold velvet on our couches that she wanted to protect it, draping huge white sheets over it. People who visited our home often asked if we were in the middle of painting our living room. As credit to her efforts, the velvet material remained spotless, but it eventually disintegrated underneath the sheets.

In the course of our brief small talk, my date very casually took off his jacket and stretched his long, bare arms across the back of the loveseat, near the corner where I was sitting. That was it. I could see the wave of disapproval wash across my mother's face. An awkward silence filled the room, my mother's stare silently willing him to pick up his jacket and excuse himself. Whenever my mother recalled this story, she would always say, "And then this strange man comes to pick Sasha up for a date and he takes off his clothes." This was always my cue to say, "No, Mama, it was only his jacket." I thought it was a wrong move on his part, too, but not as much as my mother did. The poor guy was on his way out before the date even began.

The next guy only made it as far as the doorway, where my mother glanced at his shoes, caked with mud. In my country, one could tell a lot about a person by looking at their shoes. I was hobbling toward the door, still putting on one of my sandals, when she informed him that he had the wrong address and shut the door in his face. Clearly, he did not know the old Yugoslav saying, "Look at the shoes, and only then let him in the house." How a man's shoes could be covered in mud in a concrete jungle like New York City I didn't know, but I was still willing to give him a chance. Not my mother.

My efforts at school were more rewarding than my dating life. I took American History 101 and learned about Woodrow Wilson and the two Roosevelts. I used a special pen that had four colors of ink to mark words in my English dictionary. In the margins, I jotted all kinds of phrases and additional notes for each word, using the various colors of inks. On campus, I carried the dictionary with me so I could point to words on the pages and ask people to help me pronounce them correctly. Each week, I learned something new. My English was improving, although I still wrestled daily with words and phrases that had more than one meaning; my struggle became especially embarrassing when I went to a hairstylist for the first time.

When we first lived in New York, I continued to cut my own hair, as I had done my whole life to that point. I had perfected my no-frills style by hanging my head upside down in front of the open oven door in our kitchen to dry my hair. However, now that I was in America, I felt I should do what Americans do. I'd overheard several girls in my class talk about getting their hair styled at a salon. This was in the days of the pageboy style—the Dorothy Hamill ice-skating craze. I made an appointment at a nearby salon, tucking a photo of Dorothy that I'd clipped from a magazine into my pocket to show the stylist.

Tony, the male stylist, worked an inordinate amount of time styling my hair. When he finished, he spun the chair around just like I was Dorothy in a camel spin so I could see the mirror. I was thrilled to see the spitting image of a blonde Dorothy Hamill looking back at me! Later that day, just before my next class started, I slipped into my seat, running my fingers through my new hairdo and raving to my best friend Antonia Vizcarando that Tony had just given me a "blow job." Several classmates overheard what I'd said and began to snicker. I had no idea why they were laughing, but whatever I had said became the campus joke for the next six months. People I barely knew would stop me and ask, "Do you still like blow jobs?" or "Now, who gave it to you again?" Oblivious to their sarcasm, I was pleased that they liked my hair and regularly gave out Tony's name and number.

I learned to respect how difficult it is to learn a second language. Even now, I always point out to my children that people who don't speak English very well often know at least one more language than the people making fun of them. Learning English is more difficult than people think. They deserve respect for their efforts to learn another language—*your* language.

Another time, when I was getting lunch at the school cafeteria, I saw the people in line ahead of me ordering chicken legs with green peas and potatoes. I thought it looked delicious, and I strained to understand how they ordered it. I could hear "green peas" and what sounded like "leg," but I wasn't sure of the adjective before "leg." What kind of leg was it? I didn't know. My turn in line was coming up quickly as I pushed my empty tray along. In situations like this, my primary goal was to blend in at all costs. If I did not know exactly how to say something, I would say it quickly and mumble.

Just say something close to the right word, I assured myself. *No one will ask.*

"What will you have?" the cafeteria girl wanted to know, tugging at her hairnet and wiping her brow with the back of her hand. She was impatient, moving people through the line with breakneck speed.

Quick now, act like you know what you're doing. "I'll have the children leg," I mumbled in my best American accent, following up with a last-minute shoulder shrug to indicate confidence and all the while silently pleading with her not to expose me for a fraud.

By the look on her face, I knew immediately she was not in the mood to work with me on this. She then did what I dreaded most. She stopped serving and said, "Excuse me?"

I froze.

Steady now, almost there....try something else, fast! "Oh," I said casually. "May I have the... kitchen leg?" running my words all together in an unintelligible mess.

"The what?" Her voice escalated and so did her impatience. I was breaking into a sweat. The room began to spin.

Don't panic. Blend. Blend. Blend! Finally, I tapped on the glass with my finger and urgently pointed to the chicken piece. "That! I want that!" My shout, coated with a heavy Slavic accent I could no longer disguise, reverberated through the cafeteria.

Stunned, she put a piece of chicken on my plate. I grabbed it from her hand, slid it onto my tray and hurried out of there.

I still occasionally stumble through social situations with my English today, although I like to think of my errors as being more sophisticated these days. A few years ago, I had a neuroma removed from my foot and had to quit exercising for a while. I was talking to a colleague at work, complaining about the fact that I was getting so lazy without my exercise routine. Suddenly, I noticed him looking at me funny.

Thinking he did not hear me, I repeated the last phrase I had just said. "I'm such a slut."

His alarm grew exponentially. "What did you say?"

"You know, I'm such a slut."

"No, you're not!" he interrupted.

"I know what I am! Just look at me…I don't run, I don't walk. I just sit around on the couch these days. I'm a slut!"

He seemed relieved to tell me that I meant "slug," not "slut." My vocabulary increased by two words that day. However, after he left, I spent the next thirty minutes in sheer terror trying to recall how many other people—and patients—I'd told I was a "slut."

* * *

I GRADUATED from Lehman College in three-and-a-half years with a double major in biology and psychology. Lehman offered me a scholarship to attend graduate school. I wanted to go to medical school, which my mother knew, and work with leprosy patients—which I made sure my mother never knew. She was still opposed to the idea. As an undergraduate, I had taken science courses so that I could fulfill all the prerequisites for medical school without having to declare that I was pre-med—a sure giveaway that I was still planning to be a doctor.

My mother was probably the only parent in America who didn't want her child to go to medical school. Whenever I would bring it up, her response was always the same. "Why can't you pursue a classier job like a psychologist or a professor? What's wrong with that, Sasha?" she would say, rubbing her forehead as if the very thought brought on a migraine.

She wanted me to be a teacher instead, because she believed that the power of reaching people was not in one's hands but in one's voice. To her, it was all about ideas and how to communicate them. Madame Regout used to shake her head and say, "Your mother—she has too many ideas." But my mother crossed an ocean for her ideas.

Mama had lost her job at CETA by the time I graduated from Lehman because the work-for-funds program had disbanded. It turned out that not that many people on welfare, except my mother, really wanted to work; they wanted the money, but they didn't want to work for it. The office manager put a pink slip in her box at the end of the day and that was that. She brought home the little slip of paper for me to see. She didn't understand what it meant, or didn't believe it, so she showed up for work the next day as usual. When she arrived, she made a horrible discovery. All that remained in the entire office suite were a few trash cans scattered across a barren floor. Her desk, all the chairs and tables—it had all disappeared as if it had never existed.

Up to that point, Mama was a workaholic, happily completing her assignments and everyone else's work because she didn't mind doing it and they didn't mind letting her, either. My mother had a philosophy about the value of work, something she must have adapted from Gandhi's writings. Gandhi wrote, "Live like you may die tomorrow and learn like you will live forever." My mother personalized it to reflect her own beliefs. She would often tell me, "Sasha, live like you may die tomorrow, but *work* like you will live forever."

My mother preferred any kind of work that engaged her mind to menial labor. Nevertheless, that's what she did for years with the Jesuits and in Brussels. She had the unique ability to see the connection between what you *wanted* to do versus what you *had* to do at the moment. We were willing to do what we had to do so that we could one day do what we wanted to do. That is how we made it to America.

Today, I've tried to incorporate my mother's philosophy into my own approach to work. I often tell people I don't have a job description, even though I am an oncologist by profession. If something needs to be done at work, I do it, no matter what it is. For example, I don't need to call someone from the hospital cleaning crew to clean up a small spill when I can grab a towel and clean it up myself. I will change a burned out bulb in the waiting room if I see one, and I always keep a box of light bulbs nearby for that reason. Although my mother never enjoyed the menial labor we performed over the years in Yugoslavia, she did what she had to do. And because she did, I now have the chance to do what I most wanted to do—be a doctor.

After she lost her job at CETA, she turned to her artwork with insatiable energy once again. She began painting scene after scene of our life in Yugoslavia with precise detail, as if turning over postcards in her mind and capturing them on canvas.

I think she was trying to find herself again, because all her self-worth had come from her job at CETA. For years, my mother's entire identity had fit in a plastic bag—the one containing all our legal documents. Wherever we moved in Yugoslavia, the officials would ask us who we were. And my mother would show them the bag. Everything inside that bag told us and everyone else who we were. When we moved to Austria, and for the four years we were stateless in Belgium, everyone asked the same question: "Who are you?" My mother produced the bag to show them who we were. We were nothing and no one apart from what was inside of it.

Long after we made a permanent life for ourselves in America, she continued carrying the tattered plastic bag with her any time she left home. We finally got a brown canvas bag for everything, and I have vivid memories of her slinging the heavy load over her shoulder while shopping at the flea market or a garage sale, shifting its weight from one shoulder to the other. Something instinctively told us that if we ever lost that bag, we would lose who we were.

We didn't turn to the outward makings of success to know who we were—designer clothes or the abundance of possessions. In fact, my mother never wore makeup until she was dead. The funeral home put it on her, and I hardly recognized who she was. Throughout her life, she was not particularly feminine and never wore nail polish or styled her hair. There was no reason for her to cover up who she was on the inside.

"If you're good enough, it will shine through," she would always say.

She was. And it did.

*   *   *

EVERYONE HAD told me how difficult it was to get into medical school, even for those who were born in America, so how could I expect to get in? I had heard all the nerve-racking stories about brilliant students being turned down and having to go to school in Mexico or Italy. I was terrified I might be one of them. One day, I told one of my professors about my goal of attending medical school, and he bluntly informed me that I would never get in. End of discussion.

Because I was so afraid of rejection, I decided to start taking baby steps toward applying to medical school. First, I applied to twelve dental schools and told myself that if I could get into a dental school then I could surely get into a medical school. I was accepted at all twelve and passed the dental entrance exam. I took that as a sign and began making formal application to medical school and studying for my MCATS. Much of what I was earning from tutoring and working at the hospital helped pay for the growing mountain of application fees.

Although I did not necessarily want to go to graduate school, I didn't want to lose the scholarship I'd received from Lehman College either, which is exactly what would happen if I did not enroll in a graduate program within the year. I decided to send out applications for both. When I applied for medical school, I sent out a smattering of applications across the nation to several schools I'd heard about. I did not realize that some of them would not even consider an out-of-state resident. When I applied for graduate school programs, I did the same thing and only applied to high-profile schools I'd heard other people talking about with enthusiasm. I applied and was accepted for an extremely competitive Masters/PhD program in clinical psychology at Howard University. However, I mistakenly thought I had applied to Harvard! Howard, Harvard— they both sounded the same to my untrained, non-American ear. When I accepted Howard's offer, I did not realize I had enrolled in a traditionally all-black university.

Nevertheless, I considered my acceptance into this fine program as another favorable sign that I would be able to get into medical school one day. However, Howard's graduate program was in Washington, DC, and I wasn't sure how Mama would take the news.

To my surprise, my mother packed my bags in a flash. I'd never seen her move so quickly. *How wonderful*, she thought.

A psychology program—my daughter, the psychologist. She assumed that my decision to move to DC meant that I had finally rid myself of my desire to work with bodily secretions.

She also initially assumed she would move with me, but I discouraged her, saying I would be going to school full time and focusing solely on my studies. Although she would miss me terribly, she agreed to stay in New York, drawing comfort from the fact that I was finally coming around and pursuing a real career in a field she approved.

* * *

IN ONE OF my classes at Howard, Professor Zimmerman and I were the only Caucasian faces. The school officials told me I had to live off campus because of "racial tension," a phrase I had never even heard before. I thought it had to do with something regarding the building code, and assumed that once the administration fixed the "tension" in the buildings I would be able to move to a dorm on campus. Meanwhile, I had to walk two miles every day to and from my dorm room on the campus of nearby Trinity College.

At the time, I didn't think much of the disparity between my classmates and me because I had always been different. I had never fit in. However, many of the other black students were suspect of me. "You're the token white girl," they would say, referring to quotas the administration had to fill. Others were more curious about me than anything, like one guy who asked me out on a date.

"You're not my type," I said to him.

"Why is that, because I'm black?" he said, stiffening his shoulders and preparing for a debate.

Because you're black? I thought to myself. That wasn't it at all. I just couldn't get past his unpleasant personality. However, it was the seventies, and everything seemed to be tainted with this "racial tension."

One time a girl was finishing some fried chicken out in the courtyard before class. I asked her where she got it, and she shared a complicated set of directions that led through a bad part of town. I must have walked half a dozen blocks before I saw the steps leading down to this corner dive where they sold the chicken. As soon as I walked in, a big black man met me at the door, blocking my way. "What are you doing here, honkey? You're in the wrong neighborhood."

I could not understand why he called me a monkey. Sure, I was a little out of place, but a monkey? Come on. Thankfully, an even larger black woman stood up for me and let me come in. Later, I learned he wasn't calling me a monkey at all; it was slang for a white person. Then I understood.

I once made the mistake of bringing a classmate a bag of cough drops from Yugoslavia. He had been suffering with a cough all week and, eager to make new friends, I grabbed a bag from home to share with him.

"I have something for you," I told him. "Close your eyes and hold out your hands." I proudly placed the bag in his palms. He looked at the package and his bright smile faded from his coffee-colored skin.

"Can you believe it? They're all the way from Yugoslavia," I announced proudly, pointing to the package and beaming.

In Yugoslavia, a popular brand of cough drops advertises a chimney sweeper covered in soot. He cleans your throat like a chimney with these drops. In my country, the little pieces of black licorice-like candy were called, "Negroes," as was clearly displayed on the package. Fortunately, he realized that I had no clue what I had done. He took it well, and I even kept the bag to tease him from time to time about my mistake.

* * *

MEANWHILE, I passed the MCATS and started interviewing for medical school. I bought a winter gray suit and a new pair of small heels that gave me such pain I could barely concentrate on the questions the interviewers asked me. I traveled for interviews to Albany, Rochester, Columbia and other places, without my mother ever knowing.

However, I was very discouraged because every medical school I talked to was astronomically expensive. The first interview question was often something about how I was planning to finance my education. I had no idea. Johns Hopkins had me on a waiting list, but I could not begin to afford it. At that time a student could borrow up to $50,000, but that amount would cover only the first two years' tuition. That's when I learned about an "army school," the Uniformed Services University of the Health Sciences in Maryland. They were building a new program at Bethesda Naval Hospital for the class of 1979, where students could attend medical school free in return for their service. I decided to add it to the list of schools I was considering and went for an interview.

When I was in college in New York, I had met a Slovenian friend named William. He was the one who encouraged me during this whole ordeal of applying and interviewing for medical school. When we first met, I was doing a study in clinical psychology and needed a subject for a short-term memory test. I saw a man walking by one day who looked nothing like a fellow student, with his cashmere coat and Wall Street Journal tucked under his arm.

Intrigued by his professional appearance, I asked him if he would participate in a brief study. Even though he promptly failed the memory test, I ran into him again by coincidence months later, and we developed a friendship based on our mutual interest in medicine and our similar backgrounds. He drove me from New York to Howard University in DC, and laughed uproariously when he realized I had not known Howard and Harvard were different schools.

He was brilliant and wealthy, but he wondered if he had the grades to get into medical school. He knew my situation with my mother, so we encouraged each other to overcome the odds against us and pursue our dreams anyway. "But what if my mother finds out I'm applying to medical school?" I would ask him, terrified at the proposition of her discovering my secret.

"It will be okay," he would assure me. He knew my mother, and even though she wasn't too fond of him, having deemed him a "Gypsy" the first time she met him, he constantly reminded me not to worry about her. If I got into medical school, my mother would be just fine.

She wasn't fine.

CHAPTER NINE

I'm In The Army Now

W hen I was not in class at Howard University, I was working at the Children's Hospital in DC as a nurse. I worked weekends, holidays, night shifts—whatever I could do to earn money and gain more experience. My mother was also sending me money for room and board each month. I never told her I had a nursing job at the hospital. I still did not have a checking or savings account and literally tucked all of my money under my mattress at night.

After several months, I managed to save a significant amount of money. One day, I decided to splurge on a new pair of tennis shoes at a local sport store. When I walked to the store it was closed, but I noticed there was a car dealership next door. The front row of cars in the lot had bright signs on the dashboards advertising their specials. I wandered over to have a look, and one petite silver car in the corner caught my eye. The style was an Audi Fox, and I instantly fell in love with its boxy shape and cute little side mirrors.

I walked into the front office and asked the Iranian sales-man behind the desk if the little gray car was for sale.

"Madame, everything in this lot is for sale," he replied. I'm sure he was thinking he had a real sucker on the line.

I explained to him that I liked the car, but I did not have a driver's license. I had failed a driver's test in DC and Mary-land because I could not parallel park. He said that was no problem. Someone from their staff could accompany me to Virginia to retake the test there because they did not require parallel parking.

"If you go at the end of the day, just before closing, you'll sail right through," he assured me.

The next thing I knew, an orange Pinto pulled up with an Iranian mechanic inside to ride with me across the Virginia border to pass my driver's test.

"You drive. I give directions," he said in broken English.

The driver's door would not open, so I had to climb across the passenger seat. Many a driver before me had left grease spots where their shoes had dug into the upholstery climbing across the seats. The entire car seemed like it was held together with bubble gum and the engine stuttered and spat all the way there. The broken speedometer flickered at the bottom of the dial, registering zero as we raced down the highway. It was my first experience driving in America, and I had no idea how fast I was going.

We arrived just before closing, as planned. The clerk, irritated that it was so late in the day, pointed me to the parking lot. I climbed across the passenger seat of the Pinto and into the driver's seat. She sat beside me. I drove forward a few feet, and then she gathered up her clipboard and reached for the door handle.

"You pass," she sighed, getting out of the car and motioning for me to follow her inside.

Dumbfounded, I stood across from the raised counter as she typed my information into the computer, noting my name and address.

"Hair color?" she asked.

"Blonde."

She peered over her glasses resting on the end of her nose. "That is not blonde," she countered, examining my hair. "It's mousy brown."

I tried to explain to her that my hair, while perhaps on the brown side now, lightened up in the summer—especially when I put lemon juice on it. She was not the least bit interested. She typed something. I hoped it would be "blonde."

"Eye color?"

"Green."

She took another doubtful look over her glasses, muttered something about my eyes being gray and continued typing. I was horrified at the thought that my first driver's license would say, "Mousy brown hair with dull gray eyes."

The woman laminated my license and handed me the still-warm plastic card. I clutched it to my chest without reading it, hoping to delay the disappointment of what it said.

Once I was outside, I stopped and looked. My photo had the expression of someone who had just won the lottery, and in some ways I felt I had. I was "blonde" with "green eyes" and I could now legally drive us home. Quickly, I turned around to mouth "thank you," but I saw only her back after she locked the office door and pulled the shade. I was so excited as I started the Pinto to drive back home. I don't know if it was the broken speedometer or the rush of adrenaline from receiving my driver's license, but I felt like I was flying all the way back to DC.

When we arrived at the sales lot, I bought the silver Audi Fox—in cash—and the salesman handed me my keys. My second (legal) drive in America took place that afternoon as I made my way down Pennsylvania Avenue in rush hour traffic. I nervously hustled through three yellow lights in a row before I saw the colorful lights of a police officer's car twinkling behind me. I panicked and kept driving until I heard a deep male voice on the loudspeaker, "Pull over."

I pulled over between a subway exit and a bus stop as dozens of people stared at me in my little Audi Fox. *Would they send me to jail? Can they send me back to Yugoslavia?* I was petrified.

The officer came to my window and told me I had burned through three red lights, to which I silently agreed. He gave me a ticket—only a warning. As he was leaving, he looked at my dashboard and noticed the oil light was on.

"Have you put oil in this car?"

"No, I just bought it," I explained.

"Open the hood," he ordered.

The hood? What part of the car was the hood—the front or back? I quickly scanned the instrument panel, looked under the seat and even gave the glove compartment a peek, but it was no use.

Hood. Hood. Hood? I was clueless. Suddenly, he poked his hairy arm through the window, brushing my leg as he reached for the lever next to the seat to pop the hood. I sat motionless as his hand passed the outside of my thigh, certain he was about to rape me in front of all these people.

He checked the oil, which was seriously low, and told me to fill it and check the level each time I got gas. To be extra careful, I began adding oil each time I bought gas—a little here, a little there. One day I saw a trail of blue smoke in my rearview mirror. I thought the black station wagon behind me was on fire, only to discover it was my car billowing smoke. Four hours and several hundred dollars later I learned, paraphrasing the words of the rough blue-collar mechanic at the local repair shop, that I had purchased a piece of foreign "waste matter."

"Go buy an American car," he said and lit up a cigarette in his greasy black hands.

* * *

AFTER SIX MONTHS at Howard University, the admissions officer for Uniformed Services University of the Health Sciences called my mother's apartment in New York to tell me I had been accepted into their medical school program in Bethesda, Maryland. I had not answered at my dorm in DC because I was at work. My mother picked up the phone. The official on the other end of the line wasted no time congratulating my mother on my acceptance to medical school and willingness to serve my country.

On my application, I had checked "no preference" when it asked for my preferred branch of service. I had no idea what any of them were. So, he explained to my mother, he was calling to determine what branch of service I wanted to go into—Army, Navy, Air Force or Public Health?

I can imagine my mother standing there holding the phone to her ear, reeling from the news and devising a million different ways to kill me. She asked only one question. "Well, sir," she spoke calmly, "if this was your daughter, what would you pick?"

He told her Public Health because they usually don't go to war (except by presidential appointment).

"Put her down for that," Mama said and hung up the phone.

My mother called me when I got home from work and had more than a few questions for me. For one thing, she knew nothing about my application to medical school. For another, neither of us had any idea what Public Health was. It was an uncomfortable, long conversation about what else I was hiding from her, and her paranoia kicked in at a new level. That night, she went to bed and had another long conversation. This one was with St. Jude, the patron saint of miracles. She had become super religious since I'd left home, and talked to him with the regularity of a family member.

She bought novenas, devotions consisting of prayers to obtain special graces. That night, she prayed to St. Jude to get her daughter out of this medical school predicament I'd somehow gotten myself into. If he could not do that, then if he could move her to DC or send me back to New York that would be sufficient. She could take it from there.

Regardless, the army officer called me back at my dorm soon after, instructed me to hold my right hand in the air and commissioned me as a Public Health officer over the phone. I was twenty-eight years old.

* * *

THAT JUNE I quit the program at Howard and left my job at the Children's Hospital to go for summer naval training at a merchant marine base in Kings Point, New York. I was an ensign, a junior officer, and wore the same uniform as the U.S. Navy. My mother liked the black and white uniform, although she hinted that green would have looked better on me—but the Navy had not asked her for her opinion. I learned to navigate a ship on the East River from Kings Point to Manhattan and back. Next, I served as a Public Health inspector in Norfolk, examining all the incoming ships from various countries for rats. I also inspected restaurants and served in Public Health at a women's prison that summer, gaining a variety of experience in the field.

That fall, I moved into the BOQ (Bachelors Officer Quarters) next to the Naval Hospital in Bethesda. After I lived on the naval base for six months, my mother moved from New York to DC, and I moved with her into a townhouse with a view of a beautiful green lawn across the street. We thought it was a golf course. However, when my mother discovered it was actually a cemetery, we immediately moved farther down the street to a high-rise apartment called the Pavilion "to get away from the bones." She had once worked in the water department at New York City, fueling her concerns that the nearby decomposing bodies were contaminating the water supply.

At first, she did not approve of my having a car without her knowledge, but she soon changed her mind. One, she realized it didn't kill me. Two, she loved going to the garage sales and flea markets on Saturdays. I remember her sitting in the passenger seat, calling out the addresses from the newspaper ads she'd circled earlier that morning as we searched for the sales. A friend she'd met at one of the flea markets offered to let her buy a space to sell little trinkets. My mother would buy linens and jewelry to resell, and she loved setting up her folding table and meeting people throughout the day.

""What does your daughter do?" they would sometimes ask her.

"She works with people," she would say, intentionally leaving out the fact that I was studying to become a doctor, and quickly change the subject.

During my internship, I worked on call every other night and would come home exhausted. My mother sensed I had grown independent of her and that depressed her. "The sadness of you leaving me will kill me one day," she once told me. However, I would *never* have left her. *Never.*

I was just too tired and too busy to make more effort at keeping her company. I was relieved when she eventually joined a senior citizens' activity group and began to connect with other people. I did not necessarily have close friends at medical school. Outside of the friendships I had maintained with Dominique from Brussels and William, who was now studying to be a doctor in Grenada, I did not have a lot of time to nurture relationships.

I found an emotional connection to my patients, as if they were my extended family. From the beginning, I was deeply interested in who they were outside of what their diagnosis told me about them. My mother was like that. She loved people and was truly interested in them. I remember one day going to a garage sale at a little house on top of a hill in Maryland. Slowly making their way up the narrow steps ahead of us was a man with a horrible limp and a woman in traditional, brightly colored African dress. When we reached them, my mother tapped him on the shoulder and said, "Either go faster or move over." I was embarrassed, but my mother was only being practical.

To my surprise, the man was not insulted in the least. He just smiled and said, "I would love to go faster, but I have a wooden leg."

My mother's ears perked up at this revelation. Still only halfway up the stairs, Mama stopped and insisted, "Let me see it." Something about my mother's genuine interest in strangers disarmed their usual defenses. It's not that she didn't respect the self-protective layers or boundaries most people have in place—she just never even saw them. She could worm her way into a person's business without the slightest hint of being nosy. In fact, more often than not they welcomed her in.

"Okay," the man said and bent down to roll up his pants leg. "I'm sorry. I'm so sorry," I apologized to the other shoppers impatiently passing us on the stairs.

His "prosthesis" was only a crude peg of carved wood with a shoe on the end. Mama burst out laughing. "This is like Captain Hook in the movies!" she cried. Incredibly, the man chuckled at my mother's forthrightness, too.

I wanted to die right then and there.

"Well," she said, her face serious now, "how did you get a wooden leg?" The man shared that he and his wife were from Zambia. He had lost his leg when he ran into the street after his son's soccer ball and was hit by a car.

Mama told the man about a story she'd seen on television about a soldier who received a plastic prosthesis after losing both his legs. The clear, see-through material looked like bionic legs with all the screws and hinges visible. "With one of those," Mama assured the man, "you can walk, run and even swim." Then she added almost off-handedly, "And I'm going to help you get one." No one except Mama knew how serious she was in that moment.

We finally made it up the stairs, and after a quick look around at the garage sale, she said to the man's wife, "There's nothing here. I want you to come to my house. I have clothes you can just have." Driving in my car on the way to our apartment, we discovered more about these strangers from Africa. He was a graduate student and she was a translator with the embassy. When we got home, Mama wrote down all their information and promised to be in touch. When they left, they carried two large plastic bags full of the clothes we gave them.

In the meantime, she took it upon herself to contact the United Way and arrange for the man to be measured for a prosthetic leg, which cost five thousand dollars. My mother had always saved constantly, and we paid two-thirds of the cost using my mother's savings and my meager salary.

After he received his prosthesis, he and his wife came over to our apartment to show us and thank my mother for all her help. In the middle of telling her how appreciative he was, she waved her hand, stopping him mid-sentence. "I want you to run!" she urged him. "Just like in the commercial." She stepped back and crossed her arms as he quickly walked a few paces in our tiny living room. A smile of satisfaction crept across her mouth and she nodded.

"That's all I wanted to see. Now you can go," she told him and walked them to the door. We never heard from the couple again. My mother always said to me, "Whenever you feel you should do something for someone else, you should do it. Because you may never have another chance."

* * *

IN MY SECOND year at medical school, I switched from the Public Health branch of service to the Army because the Public Health program was closing down. They closed the hospital in Carville, Louisiana, which had been for leprosy patients. The Hawaiian island of Molokai, where Father Damien had served, was closed to the public as well. If I stayed in Public Health, I would be relegated to a few Native American tribes to treat alcoholism and tuberculosis. I did not see myself living on an Indian reservation the rest of my life, so I transferred to the Army.

The Army brought back memories of seeing firemen when I was a little kid. People smoked in movie theaters back then in Yugoslavia, so it wasn't unusual for billowy clouds of smoke to cover the movie screen while we were watching a show. Usually midway through the film, the local firemen would burst in, donned in heavy dark blue coats, because someone thought the building was on fire.

More than once, I told my mother I wanted to be a policeman or a fireman one day. I loved the sense of order these men had—not to mention the dark uniforms with two rows of shiny gold buttons and red seams. When I joined the Army, I felt it was a good fit with my personality because I enjoyed the structure and orderliness. Every officer's quarters were the same, no matter where in the States you moved. The rank was the same. The pay was the same. After a lifetime of relative chaos, I kept coming back to the comfort of a routine where I knew exactly what to expect.

At the same time, I had grown into a devoted patriot. I've often said that only a non-American can fully appreciate America. In fact, the song, "I'm Proud to Be an American" could have been written for me. I was ready to serve my new country and support America as a member of the armed services. I was grateful to the Army for the opportunity they gave me to go to medical school—just as grateful as I was to the Jesuits for helping us and to the Catholic Church for helping me go to school in Brussels and come to America. I owed each of them so much and wanted to make sure I made something of myself as a result of their generosity.

* * *

I GRADUATED from medical school in 1983. In 1985, I was a second-year resident at Walter Reed Army Hospital. I met some wonderful people, including Dr. Rafenstein, the Chief of Cardiology in the Navy. In late summer that year, he was caring for his wife who'd had a stroke. His wife stayed in the hospital a while, but eventually died. I hit it off with the Rafenstein family immediately and grew quite close to their son, who lived in Alaska. He worked as a chef on a ferry, although he had a graduate degree, and his wife owned two bookstores in Juneau. That September, they invited me for a visit, even going so far as to make a ferry reservation for me so I would know their offer was sincere.

I did not tell my mother I was going to Alaska, because she would have been upset. Earlier that spring, I had moved out and was living with one of my classmates from school. The separation was difficult at first, but I felt I needed some time apart from her and the strict rules she still placed on me. I was thirty-four years old, yet she still wouldn't let me date as long as I lived under her roof. I couldn't even wear makeup. I was tired of feeling guilty each time I secretly ran some lip gloss over my lips in the elevator on the way to the hospital. A little time apart, I thought, would be best for both of us.

I flew to Seattle and boarded a ferry on a Friday for the journey through beautiful Vancouver, planning to spend the next three days with my friends in Juneau, Alaska. That Friday was my mother's birthday, September 20. Mama and I never celebrated any special occasions, including our birthdays. Because of the transient nature of our lives when I was growing up, there was no time to build family traditions. My mother usually just asked me prior to my birthday what I needed and gave it to me.

Friday night on the ferry, I wrote in my journal. I do not usually journal, but my mother's friend had given me one and I felt obligated to use it. I settled into my seat on the ferry and smoothed the first page with my hand. I dated the paper September 20, 1985. *This is my mother's birthday, 1923–1985*, I wrote underneath.

Chills ran down my spine when I read the words. For some reason, I wrote the dates as if I were reading a tombstone. I quickly took my pen and added, "This means she is 62 today." Just to clarify this horrible thought. Was I predicting my mother's death somehow? When I was a child, I had a dream that my great-grandfather Svetislav had died. I woke up screaming and Mama rushed into my room. I described his coffin in detail—it had a red, velvety cloth inside. My mother dismissed my fears. "It's just a dream, Sasha. You go back to sleep."

The next day, we received a telegram informing us that Svetislav had died during the night. When we went to visit the family during the week of the funeral, we walked into the room and saw that the inside of his coffin was lined with red velvet.

* * *

WHEN I arrived at the Rafenstein's home later that same day, I learned my mother had died. Her physician had phoned my roommate, who had contacted the Rafensteins. No one knew exactly when she died—their best guess was within the past two or three days. When she failed to show up for several appointments and meetings with friends, the police had broken through the front door of her apartment and discovered her body.

* * *

I FLEW BACK from Alaska immediately. After spending the first night at Dianka's, my first responsibility was to pick out the clothes my mother would be buried in. When I arrived at my mother's apartment door, I could see the chain was damaged where the police had broken down the door to get inside. As I fingered the chain in my hand and stepped through the doorway, I wanted to yell as I had a hundred times before, "Mama, I'm home." I noticed that her kitchen was immaculately clean. I opened the refrigerator. She had a bag of garlic bagels, some feta cheese, a few oranges and a couple of wrinkled apples. And, of course, there were eggs. We always had eggs.

The living room was also in order—neatly arranged with comfortable chairs and pillows. But the bedroom told a different story. The bed was not made and the little wicker chair next to her bed had toppled over. One of the police officers later told me he found my mother in the bed. Another said he found her *next* to the bed. I wasn't sure which one was right. Kneeling down to look more closely, I saw that the chair had dried blood and saliva mixed in the wicker border. Feeling sick to my stomach, I took a wet sponge from the bath and washed it off as best I could.

I looked around the apartment and kept replaying the scene in my head, trying to put the missing pieces together based on the evidence I saw. Sometimes I imagined she struggled to get out of the bed at the last minute and suffocated in her cries for help. At other times, I imagined it might have been sudden and painless. But no matter how "sudden" it was, it wasn't sudden enough for me. There it was again—the haunting question that I most wanted to know: "Did she suffer?" I desperately wanted to know the timeline of what happened so I could say for certain how long it was before she actually died. No one knew.

In the coming days and weeks, I would talk to everyone from the Chief of Cardiology to several neurologists, trying to figure out what happened to my mother. I constantly asked them hypothetical questions. "If my mother had a pulmonary embolism, how long would it take to die from that?" "What if it was an aneurysm—would she have felt any pain?" The questions went on and on, but no one could help set my mind at ease because no one knew exactly what had happened. I still don't know what killed my mother.

This obsession continued for years after my mother's death. I would wake up in the middle of the night, playing out scenarios in my mind about this or that—a catastrophic stroke or a hidden illness—searching for an answer and struggling to find peace.

As I squeezed the dirty water out of the sponge and into my mother's bathroom sink, I realized the merciful numbness I had felt on the flight home the day before was wearing off. The pain was back. Suddenly my eyes watered and stung; I wiped them with the back of my hand. I felt overwhelmed with loneliness again. Fortunately, this wave lasted only a few seconds. There were things to do. The funeral home was waiting on me to return with a dress for my mother to wear.

I smiled to myself as I thumbed through her clothes—dresses of every size, many still with the price tags. When she became overweight, my mother no longer paid much attention to her clothing, although at one time she was a very sharply dressed woman.

My eyes fell on a blue dress with an overcoat made of very light material. She had bought this dress just two years ago when I graduated from medical school. She had never worn it since. I rummaged around in the closet until I found the pair of shoes she had also worn at my graduation. They were burgundy with small heels and little decorative holes in the leather seams. I slipped the dress off the hanger, carefully folded it and placed it with the shoes in a brown bag and left. I wanted to get out of there.

* * *

EVERYONE thought it was a bad idea for me to see my mother dead, but I needed to do it. It would help me finally comprehend that she was really gone. Like a heavy wool coat on a summer day, I carried the stifling guilt of not being there for her when she died. Today, I go to great lengths to comfort my patients' families after they are gone because I still haven't reconciled the death of my mother. I often call or write notes to comfort families, assuring them any way I can that their loved ones are in a better place. Still, it doesn't remove one ounce of the guilt I feel for not being able to comfort my own mother when she needed me most.

The funeral home directors took me to the second floor where she was. The room was large, and I immediately recognized the coffin I had selected the day before. My mother was lying inside. Her body was so swollen she did not look like herself at all. I came closer and touched her face. She was so cold. Wanting to get closer to her, I leaned forward to kiss her forehead, but instead of the smell of her skin, I breathed in the familiar pungent scent of the other cadavers that I had worked on in anatomy lab.

The only part of her that still looked and felt like my mother was her hair: gray but still soft, although it too smelled like formaldehyde. Layers of thick makeup covered her face, making her look like a painted old lady. I looked closer and spotted that she was only wearing one clip-on earring. My mother never wore earrings, and if she had worn them, she certainly wouldn't have worn just one. Then it dawned on me that the piece of jewelry must have been in the bag that I brought her clothes in, most likely left over from one of her weekend flea markets. I smiled and gently removed the single earring and slipped it in my pocket.

I wanted to see her skin without any makeup on it, so I lifted the sleeve of her dress and saw the plastic shroud covering her wrist. I gently pushed it back and felt the cold, pale skin underneath. When I touched it, a small piece of preserved flesh came off on my fingertip. I was holding a piece of my mother's flesh in my hand. I quickly wiped my finger under the shroud, realizing in that moment that my mother's body was now like any other dead person I'd seen—cold, stiff and still.

As if she were standing over my shoulder observing this very surreal moment, I suddenly understood something my mother had always said about what makes someone who they are. It's not the size of their hips or the color of their eyes—it's the person they are inside. And that's what goes away when we die. That's what was now gone from my mother.

As I left the room, I glanced back at her profile in the casket. From that distance, she looked more like Mama. I shut my eyes like a camera lens capturing that last image. I felt like a child lost in a store—separated from my parents and terrified they would never find me. Inside I was screaming, "Mama, do not leave me…please!" I still needed her so much.

* * *

WHEN I WALKED out, my mother's friends, Dianka and her husband John, were waiting for me. Without a word, we got in the car and drove to the cemetery to choose a burial plot.

I buried her in the same cemetery with the flat headstones and green grass we had seen outside our apartment window when she first joined me in DC. I chose a place on a hill, under an oak tree. It was somewhere nice and quiet so that whenever I wanted to visit, I could sit under the full branches of that tree and talk to her.

Father Connelly gave a touching sermon at the funeral. He was a Catholic priest who served at Walter Reed on the weekends, and I had developed a friendship with him. I'd gone to him many times to talk with him about my mother and my life. He knew her well and even came over once to have dinner with us. In addition to Father Connelly, a few friends were there, but no family.

During the funeral, a little bird flew above the altar as Father Connelly spoke. Everyone was watching it as it fluttered about. In my mother's paintings, she often painted birds in flight, their opened wings dotting the landscape. I'm sure everyone there who knew my mother's paintings had their own version of what this bird's presence at my mother's funeral meant. But I laughed inside when Father Connelly said the bird was "Katarina's soul."

"It's only a bird," I told myself. Nevertheless, it eventually landed on the coffin, where it stayed throughout the ceremony. When the sermon was over, it flew away.

CHAPTER TEN

TEXAS BOUND

I cleaned out my mother's apartment and sent most of her things to Goodwill. I kept a sweater and her coat, the same coat she was wearing the night we arrived in America. It was a custom-made overcoat that we'd scrimped and saved to purchase for our big trip. I'd had one made just like it. Then I went back to working every other night on call in the Emergency Room, after having three days off to bury my mother.

The first patient on my first night back at work was DOA. She was a woman about my mother's age. It was obvious to everyone in the room that the woman was dead, but I immediately began efforts to revive her anyway, ordering fluids, shocking her heart repeatedly and following the protocol.

I coded her for what seemed like several hours, sweat pouring off my face and onto the gurney. Finally, the Chief Resident came down from his office and peeled me off the woman's body. "That's enough," he said softly yet forcefully into my ear. "That's enough."

That spring, in 1986, I was scheduled to do a rotation as a resident for two months in Kenya, East Africa. It was an elective, but it was also the fulfillment of my lifelong dream: working with leprosy patients. I was scheduled to do research at the Kenya Research Institute, a new modern research facility in the heart of Nairobi.

On my way to Africa, I flew over the Atlantic for the second time in my life. The first time, I was a stateless immigrant who spoke not a word of English. Fourteen years later, I was now traveling as an American citizen and Army doctor. However, I felt much the same way as I had all those years ago: I was on an adventure to another country and did not know what to expect.

Getting there was a challenge in itself. Initially, I was told I had to pay my own way to Nairobi, which would cost about a thousand dollars, but I knew the Navy flew cargo planes to Nairobi twice a week, every week. I challenged the policy on not allowing Army doctors to fly these regular routes. No one had ever done that before. After going back and forth a few times with officials, I soon found myself seated, facing towards the tail, in the very primitive metal seats that are inside a Navy cargo plane—bound for Africa. All around me were giant cardboard boxes and packages of supplies, strapped down with ties and cords. It cost me sixteen dollars and fifty cents, including two TV dinners.

Soon after we arrived, I began my studies at the Kenya Research Institute. However, after only two or three days in this sterile but beautiful modern facility, I realized I might as well be in Washington. I came to Africa to be in the bush, out among the people who most needed my help. I saw a chance to change my plans when I met Dr. David Bales, an infectious disease Army physician. He and his wife, Phyllis, traveled to Nairobi once a month to get their mail and then made their way to the border of Uganda to a small village called Busia, a leprosarium. Even though it would mean leaving my work at the Institute (not to mention traveling six hours by car over rough roads), I begged them to take me with them.

"It's nowhere land, Dr. Vukelja," they informed me, referring to the remote village for people with highly communicable diseases.

140

"That's where I want to go!" I insisted. It seemed that from the beginning, I had to battle uphill to come on this trip. There was always something or someone trying to talk me out of it. I sometimes wondered if it wasn't Mama somehow at work from beyond the grave.

Back in the States, before I left for Africa, I had to take a series of vaccinations, including shots for polio, yellow fever, rabies, and so forth. Two days after the polio vaccine, I was getting dressed one morning and could not button my uniform. The buttons felt clumsy in my right hand as I tried to maneuver them into the tiny holes of my shirt. I ignored it, assuming I had slept on my arm through the night and it would get better in time. However, backing out of my driveway, I was not able to grip the steering wheel tightly and ended up grazing a column by my garage. Later that day, I saw a neurologist who thought I might have a rare complication from the polio vaccine that was similar to polio itself.

The weakness and numbness in my hand eventually went away, but I remember telling myself I would get over this problem and go to Africa "if God wants me." I wasn't necessarily thinking about God, and hadn't thought of him in years. I had never attended church in America. It was more like an expression, but it caught me by surprise that God would even enter my mind.

After assuring the Bales I could handle whatever we encountered, I finally convinced them to take me with them, and I caught my breath when we pulled into the village. Next door to the tiny house where they stayed was a hospital with a four-bed infectious disease unit for patients who were severely ill. The rest of the hospital was for patients with chronic medical problems who required less intense care. Dr. Bales was studying the effects of sleeping sickness and leprosy on about two hundred patients. I was in heaven.

Most of the leprosy patients had missing limbs—no fingers, noses, hands or toes. No one in their home villages wanted to take them back, so most of them were in Busia to stay. I immediately felt at home among these exiles—mothers, fathers, daughters and sons abandoned by their own families. They were like me in so many ways. People without a home. Seeds without soil. Plants with no roots. Like useless weeds, they'd been yanked from the dirt and carelessly tossed aside.

The patients with sleeping sickness fell into a mysterious sleep for weeks at a time. We also had cases of syphilis, and numerous patients with malaria. Additionally, we encountered a new, unknown illness that, for lack of a better diagnosis, was called the "slimming disease." These patients would rapidly lose a tremendous amount of weight and then die. It was happening all over Africa that year. In the big government hospital, hundreds of them would cover the floor, just wasting away, and no one knew what to do about it. It was the beginning of the worldwide AIDS crisis—but at the time, we were unaware of what that was.

Each day started after Fibi, the Bales' housekeeper, cooked breakfast. Then I would walk over to the hospital to help run the clinics. Several times a week, we did research and ran outreach clinics sponsored by the World Health Organization to help address the epidemic of 50,000 annual cases of leprosy. Our strategy was to treat non-infected children in order to prevent the vertical transmission of leprosy from mother to child. For every child that entered the clinical trial, we agreed to take care of his or her entire family. However, in a culture where polygamy ran rampant, one child's family might include three mothers, one father and thirty siblings.

The roads to these clinics, which were stationed every fifteen to twenty miles because of the high number of cases, were marked with potholes as big as cattle. I called them "organ-prolapsing" roads because after a few bumpy hours in the truck it felt as though your stomach had dropped all the way into your big toe and your brain was now somewhere in your chest.

In these outreach clinics, I encountered everything imaginable—and some things you wouldn't want to imagine if you could! A mother brought in a young child who was burning with fever and wrapped in a thick blanket despite the sweltering heat. The child was shaking. There was no word in their dialect for "fever," so many patients would refer to everything as either a "headache" or "malaria."

Suddenly, the child writhed in her mother's arms, her torso undulating as if she was about to throw up. I quickly turned the child's head so she could vomit, but instead of food, she vomited a ball of long, white worms that had decided it was too hot inside the child. It was like *The Exorcist*, pulling these lengthy creatures out of her throat and slinging them into a basin.

At another outreach clinic, I was examining a man who was completely disrobed while a group of curious, giggling children casually looked on through a cutout in the wall. At the same time, a speckled hen crouched in a corner not three feet away from us and laid her egg, proudly announcing its arrival to all within earshot. It was chaos.

The days began early and ended late at night, but some patients still had to wait days before we could get to them. In a place that didn't have watches or calendars, they patiently agreed to line up and simply wait so they wouldn't miss their appointments.

We had limited medicines, supplies and tools, but our team

of doctors and nurses had endless tenacity and creativity to do what we could to help the people. One day, a woman came to us with a scar over her left breast and a fresh wound near what appeared to be a mass. She was asking for something sharp so she could cut out the mass herself and not have to "bother" one of the "white doctors." I may not have known all the tropical diseases we were dealing with in these African clinics, but when I saw this woman I immediately thought, *I know what she has. She has breast cancer.*

"She had that same mass last year," one of the field workers translated for me. It turned out to be an abscess, something she had removed once before by using the bottom of a glass soda bottle to carve it out of her chest. She was relieved when we lanced the mass for her and drained it.

It wasn't unusual for children to bring other children to the clinics. One time, a six-year-old traveled untold miles from her village to bring us her infant sister. With over one hundred different dialects, it was difficult to obtain any medical history and sometimes almost impossible to figure out what was wrong with the patient with such limited communication.

One little boy came to the clinic every day, wearing bright orange crocheted socks on his black feet. He sat quietly on a wooden bench all day, contentedly waiting. Nothing was physically wrong with him. He just wanted to shake hands with a white doctor. The children were all so brave, refusing to cry even when we had to give them shots or draw blood. It was a few days before I learned that the big sign outside the hospital said: "No crying and no whining allowed."

Another woman, named Grace, had been hospitalized for three months. She had given birth to her child at home and then was suddenly diagnosed with sleeping sickness. After she got better, she kept promising me a special gift, something that sounded like "gae-gae," if we would return her to her village so she could see her newborn baby. Every day it was the same thing. She would look at me with a hopeful smile and say repeatedly, "Gae-gae? Gae-gae?" I would just smile back, not knowing what she meant.

Finally, the day came when she was well enough to go home. We were busy working in the clinic that morning when suddenly this awful smell filled our nostrils. Grace was standing at the door, proudly holding a large, whole fish wrapped in newspaper—my gae-gae. I smiled and thanked her, even stopping to pose for a picture with the creature before we loaded up the four-wheel-drive truck for the three-hour journey back to Grace's village. We were taking her home, just as we promised.

One day the clinic closed early and we met for a bite to eat at a local "restaurant"—a few tables set up underneath some trees next to the water. They served us a local brand of beer called Tusker (with elephant tusks prominently displayed on the label) while we waited for our lunch and took in all the fabulous scenery. The colors of Africa are stunningly beautiful. We watched a nearby herd of hippos blowing bubbles, their snouts just barely above water and their tiny ears twitching. After a few hours, however, our lunch still had not arrived and it was beginning to get dark.

"Are we still going to eat lunch?" we tentatively asked the woman serving us.

"Yes, they're coming now!" she replied with a bright smile and pointed to the water, where a lone wooden boat was making its way to the dock, laden with the day's catch. It wasn't long before we were enjoying the freshest fish I'd ever eaten.

SEEDS

AFTER TWO months in Africa, I visited Egypt for two weeks and then returned to the States. I had very little say on where the Army would send me next, although I secretly hoped I could stay at Walter Reed the rest of my life. I never saw myself going anywhere else.

Then, one day in 1989, I ran into my new Chief, Dr. John Redmond. I was on my way up to the clinic after a meeting on the second floor. As the elevator doors opened to take me back upstairs, Dr. Redmond stepped out and said hello. I greeted him and pushed the number 7 inside the elevator. Just as the doors were closing, he suddenly turned around in the hallway, stuck his foot between the doors and said, "Think about Texas."

"Why?" I said.

"Because I'm thinking about sending you there."

Then the doors closed.

I was stunned. I eventually reached my floor, but I didn't get off. I couldn't move. I went up and down the elevator as people came in and went out, but I just stood there frozen. Texas? The only immediate comfort I had was that I had seen several episodes of Bonanza. I loved Hoss and Little Joe, although Hoss was my favorite. My mind filled with flashbacks of watching that show with my mother and several neighbors gathered in our living room in Yugoslavia. They brought chairs over to our home to watch it, because we were lucky enough to have the only television in the neighborhood. Gathered around the tiny set, we engrossed ourselves in this weekly television drama, the "magic of television" blurring the line between what was real and imaginary. When Little Joe called for a doctor in one of the episodes, the young son of a neighbor pointed to his dad, who was a physician, and blurted out, "The doctor is here!" Watching a scene set in the local saloon one day, a neighborhood teenager got up from his chair and walked around the back of the set, trying to "peer" down at the alluring cleavage of one of the saloon girls.

Despite the warm memories I had of Bonanza, I did not want to live in Texas. My instinct was to start gathering information immediately, looking for a way to get out of my assignment. I was doing great at Walter Reed. I was a fellow in hematology and oncology, and I was publishing. They loved me there. I had never entertained the slightest possibility that I might leave. The people I talked to about my plight weren't helping. "They own you," they told me. "They paid for your education—they can send you anywhere they want!" Others tried to comfort me by saying things like, "Texas is not so bad. It could be worse—they could send you somewhere you couldn't even pronounce!" I wasn't feeling any better.

Within three months, I was packing my things for the move to San Antonio. The day the Army's movers arrived, I ran into my next door neighbor, a Jewish psychologist, for the first time in five years. We just happened to be in the hallway as he was coming home and the movers were hauling out another load of boxes from my place.

"You must be my neighbor," he said and shook my hand.

"Not anymore, because I'm going to Texas," I said, barely disguising the disappointment in my voice.

"Oy vay, Texas!" he said and rubbed his curly beard with his thumb and forefinger. He had beady little eyes and was wearing a blue wool cardigan over a plain white shirt.

"Do you know anything about Texas?" I asked hesitantly, afraid of what I might hear.

"Let me tell you about *Texas*," he said with a hush, leaning in as if to tell me a big secret. *"Those* people…" he paused, looked from side to side and leaned in a bit further. "Those people are so primitive that they actually put their family's initials on cows' buttocks."

I was horrified. He nodded, greatly satisfied by my response. A mover stepped around me in the hallway, taking another load of boxes out the door to the truck. My neighbor unlocked his door and stood in the doorway to continue our conversation.

"Really?" I was beginning to feel nauseous.

"And another thing…" he said with the seriousness of someone in his profession. "The roaches are so big they fly like birds." He held out his hands about a foot wide and raised his curly eyebrows up and down.

He saw all the color draining from my face and realized that he was not helping the situation. He quickly added with a smile, "But the good thing about Texas is that they refill your iced tea for free!" With that, he closed his door.

I stood there in shock, thinking to myself, *I don't even drink iced tea.*

* * *

I LEFT FOR San Antonio as soon as the truck was packed. I drove all the way from DC to Texas, armed with two cassette tapes of Roy Orbison and John Denver—my attempt at listening to country music. I'd bought them at a gas station on the way down and listened to "Pretty Woman" and "Take Me Home, Country Roads" about 45 times each. Whenever I flipped sides, I held the steaming hot plastic cassette outside my sunroof trying to cool it off, but burned up my car stereo anyway by the time I crossed the Texas border.

By now, I was driving a new car. My poor Audi Fox would never have made it to Texas. In fact, right after my experience with the blue smoke coming out of the tailpipe, I took my mechanic's advice and bought an American car. I wasn't entirely sure what an American car meant, but I could not afford to take my Audi into the shop every two weeks.

After work one day, I walked into another car dealership that had a big sign with the word, "Ford" on it and asked, "Is this an American car lot?" I'm sure alarms went off for the salesman sitting behind his desk, and he was thinking he had a real "winner" on the line.

"It sure is," he said and jumped up to shake my hand.

I saw a silver sports car with a red interior parked prominently in front and it reminded me of my little silver Fox. I pointed to it and said, "I would like to buy that one." He said it was a Mustang—which I inevitably called a Moostang the rest of the night.

The salesman pulled out a drawer in his desk and started searching for the keys. "Would you like to test drive it?"

Now the alarms were going off in *my* head because I was afraid he thought I was this poor little foreign woman with an accent. I had no idea how the song-and-dance between a car salesman and a customer worked. Although he was just trying to be nice, I stiffened and countered, "Why do I have to test drive it? Is there something wrong with the car that you're not telling me?"

Fearful that he was about to lose an easy sale, he quickly recovered. "No, no, there's nothing wrong with the car. In fact, I'll take $500 off the price right now."

Instead of making me feel better, that made me even more suspicious! Why was he coming down on the price? Surely there *was* something wrong with it! My accent grew thicker with my increasing anxiety. "Are you trying to give it away because no one wants it?" I asked, hands on hips.

He finally realized that I needed help to see that he was actually doing me a favor. He coaxed me to sit down so he could explain more thoroughly. After a while, we agreed on a price. I started to relax again, as did he, and we began the paperwork.

"Now, Sasha, how are you going to pay for the car?" he asked.

"With money!" I said matter-of-factly, patting a wad of the cash that I was still stashing under my mattress at night. The paranoia kicked in again. *What did he think I was going to use?*

He looked up at me blankly, took a deep breath and finished the paperwork without another word. I traded in my Audi Fox, paid my money and walked out that day with the keys to a new American-made Moostang. Life was great—until it broke down a few months later one night on my way home from the hospital. Without warning, it just stopped. I had to walk all the way home in the dead of night in Rock Creek Park. With each step I took, I grew more determined that I would never be stranded by a car again and vowed I would buy the best-engineered car I could afford.

The next day, while I was resting at home, I saw a commercial for a Mercedes and heard the announcer call it the "best-engineered car." I immediately got up from my chair, dressed in my black uniform shoes and three-sizes-too-big gray sweat suit that I had borrowed from my mother's friend Dianka, and went to buy a Mercedes. On the way out the door, I noticed several grease spots on my sweatshirt. I was on a mission and I didn't want to take the time to change, so I just turned the sweatshirt around and continued on my way.

I entered the nearest Mercedes showroom in my backwards and baggy sweats, holding my "purse"—a yellow plastic bag from a video store that contained my wallet, stuffed with cash. I'd still never opened a checking account or a credit card. I applied for a credit card at a gas station once, but I was turned down because I'd never established credit before. I tried to explain that I was trying to establish it now, but it didn't seem to matter.

No one was in front at the Mercedes showroom, so I walked around to the side. It was late in the day and I saw a salesman eating chicken out of a box, watching TV in the break room. Apparently, he had been expecting a cleaning lady to come in for a job interview, which he promptly assumed was me after one look at my appearance.

He got up from the table and his knees crackled like popcorn popping.

"Oh, that's just my Redskins injury," he joked, but it turns out he really had played professional football for the Redskins.

"Sit down...do you want some chicken?" he offered, pushing the box toward me.

"Sure," I said and took a seat next to him as I reached in the box for a chicken wing. *This is a really friendly place*, I thought to myself as we enjoyed chicken and made small talk.

After a few minutes, he finally realized that I was not the cleaning lady after all—I was a customer! He jumped to his feet and apologized, but I already liked him so much that I didn't mind.

He showed me a custom black Mercedes that I immediately named "Black Orchid." I reached in my bag for my cash, but he kindly sat down with me and showed me how to apply for credit and finance the car.

We actually became friends that evening. He showed me how to open my first bank account. He took the time to walk me through how to fill out a check properly and spell out the numbers for various amounts. I learned to write "one-hundred" for $100 and jotted down the spellings for each number on a piece of paper that I carried in my checkbook so I would not forget.

I drove all the way to Texas in my new Black Orchid without a single incident.

* * *

WHEN I MOVED into my San Antonio apartment, which was in a nice gated community, the first thing I did was install an alarm and a triple lock on my door. I was used to living in big cities like DC and New York, where one is wary of neighbors. It never occurred to me that Texas was a different world altogether. In fact, I had not been at my new place three hours before one of my new neighbors came over, holding a plate of homemade cookies, to welcome me. When she arrived, I was in the middle of trying to figure out how I could install bars on my windows.

"I don't think you need to do that, honey," my neighbor said in a singsong voice that dripped with sugar. "This is the safest place in the world."

I had already experienced a severe blow when I discovered Bonanza was not even in Texas! Now this lady was telling me I could not install bars on my windows? My door led right into my living room—how could I protect myself? The poor guy who installed my alarm, with tight jeans and an oversized gold belt buckle, had to set and erase my alarm code three times before I trusted that he was not going to break in and steal everything that night and attack me.

Until this point of my life, whenever people had been extraordinarily nice to my mother and me I had accepted it without question. I had my mother with me—she could sniff out any danger in a heartbeat. If she was not afraid, it never entered my mind to be afraid either. Then after she died, I always lived with roommates. Now, however, I was living entirely on my own for the first time in my adult life. I was suspicious of everyone and everything. I was used to New York, where no one makes eye contact unless they have to. People live in their own little busy, serious worlds and generally mind their own business.

Contrast that to the people I met in Texas, who were friendly for no reason. I didn't know them, but they were always bringing me little gifts and stopping by to "check on me" if they hadn't seen me in a while. "What is *wrong* with these people?" I wondered to myself one night, as I found yet another jar of homemade strawberry preserves—a gift from one of my Texas neighbors—outside my door. This kind of thing would never happen in New York or DC. I stuffed the jar into a cabinet in my kitchen alongside a growing collection of other such neighborly gifts—homemade jellies and roasted pecans in bags adorned with curly ribbon. I was still suspicious as to why they went to so much trouble to be nice to someone they hardly knew.

One of my neighbors, Cathy Dolter, was a nurse at Brook Army Medical Center, where I also worked. She was also far too nice, but she eventually became a good friend of mine. She helped me realize that if I'd just relax and accept the Southern hospitality, I'd live longer. I have a quotation in my office that says, "Life is too short not to live it as a Texan." I found out how true that is when Cathy took me to my first American shopping mall. The beautiful displays of every consumer good imaginable were mesmerizing. The only thing I could settle on was a lipstick. On the way to the car, I took out my purchase and rolled the tube all the way up, trying to gauge how much was inside. Like my mother, I had to know if I'd gotten my money's worth. Suddenly, the tube of lipstick broke off at the base and fell to the pavement. I sheepishly looked at Cathy.

"Oops!"

Instead of agreeing that it served me right for being so cheap, Cathy insisted we return it and get my money back.

"It's just a lipstick, for Pete's sake, and besides it was my fault!" I told her, not wanting to cause a scene at the cosmetics counter.

Cathy would not hear of it. She marched us back into the store, where for the next ten minutes an extremely apologetic saleslady tried to make up for *my* mistake. She replaced the lipstick for free and even gave me a gift bag "for my trouble." In New York, you break it, you pay for it. Not in Texas. I seriously wondered if the salesclerk was taking the same "nice" pills everyone else seemed to be taking! I could not figure this place out.

At work, I was trying to introduce Cathy to another doctor, who was doing his residency in dermatology at Brook. I'd casually known Larry from medical school in DC because he was one year behind me and we'd been in a few study groups together. I didn't remember much about him, but he seemed like a great person. He'd already been living in Texas and working at Brook for a year or so before I arrived. "See? It's fate," I kept telling Cathy, trying to convince her that Larry would be a good match for her. In the meantime, Larry was not cooperating with my matchmaker plans for him to ask my friend Cathy out on a date. Instead, he seemed much more interested in talking to *me*.

CHAPTER ELEVEN

GOD'S ARMY

L arry asked me out to dinner one day, but I was not inclined to go. For one thing, I was his superior. He was still in his residency and, despite what you see on television dramas, hospital staff rarely socialize with those in training. Nevertheless, after much persuasion from Larry, I finally agreed to go to dinner with him one night—with the understanding that we were just former schoolmates from back East.

Part of my hesitation was that I was also starting to feel attracted to him. One of the interns on my team posted a new guy's picture on her cubicle wall every two weeks—the latest man she was madly in love with. All the nurses and doctors teased her mercilessly about the ruthless way she went through men. That was the last thing I wanted people thinking about me. I was now 39 years old and still single. I told myself that I would never be like that—putting someone's picture up one week and then another new guy's picture the next week. If I ever framed a photo of a man, it had better be someone who would *stay* in that frame.

* * *

AFTER A FEW MONTHS of living in Texas, I began to love my new life there. I rode my bike and went running several times a week on the trails that wound through my neighbor-

155

hood and nearby parks. I became very active and physically fit. It was also a rewarding period in my life professionally. I helped start the bone marrow transplant program and built a new unit where I served as Chief.

I also made more new friends, including General Bill Schneider and his wife Barbara. He was a three-star general and took it as his personal mission to introduce me to Texas. They took me to my first rodeos and familiarized me with the finer points of Southern culture. Chaplain Clark and his wife, Norma, were also good friends of mine. I was treating their daughter Elisabeth, who had cancer. Even though she did not want to undergo treatments, she taught me that sometimes doing nothing is the best treatment. Elisabeth made me a better physician, showing me that doing the smallest things may have the biggest impact on someone who is hurting. She was a young woman with great faith, and she died at home surrounded by the people who loved her.

Meanwhile, Larry and I were spending more and more time together. I was intrigued by how kind and generous he was. We shared the same philosophy about our patients. Most of all, I knew without a doubt that my mother would have liked him and said he was good for me. I'm not as gutsy as my mother was. She was a self-propelled human being who lived on autopilot most of the time. On the other hand, I need more feedback and reassurance. Larry was able to offer that; he was always quick to encourage me to follow my dreams and passions.

One day, about eight months after we'd begun seeing each other, he received notice that the Army planned to send him to Fort Devens in Boston. We were devastated. We knew the Army was not likely to let me join him in Boston anytime soon, because I was deeply involved in the transplant program. On the other hand, he was a dermatologist and could serve anywhere they chose to send him. We were told that unless we were married (being engaged did not count), the Army could not change Larry's assignment. We had three weeks to decide before he would move thousands of miles away.

I'll never forget the reaction when we decided to announce that Larry and I were getting married. All the doctors and nurses seemed happy for us—but no one had even known we were dating! General Schneider was thrilled and offered to walk me down the aisle in place of my father. There were others, however, who heard about our short-notice wedding and immediately assumed we *had* to get married. Of course, we knew that was not the case at all. In fact, after we married we had to endure three years of infertility before we had our first baby, Maxi.

To Larry's credit, he masterfully blended our two backgrounds together to form a family, starting early on with his proposal. It proved to be our first lesson in bringing our two cultures together. In my country, when a man proposed to a woman, it was customary for her to say "no" at first. The thought behind this was that the man would then beg the woman to marry him, forever proving his adoration. The older women in my country would often say to single women, "If the man is really serious, he will ask you more than once."

Truth be told, I think it's the fact that Yugoslav women liked being begged a little bit—and not just from suitors. In my country, if you visited someone's home, they often offered you homemade marmalade (served by the spoonful and followed with a glass of cold water). However, it was customary to decline their offer initially. That would give the host great pleasure to then plead with you, "Please, please. You *must* try this." Proposals worked much the same way. I learned the hard way that this was not so with marriage proposals in America.

When Larry proposed and I heard the words I'd waited 39 long years to hear, I smiled and said no, as expected, thinking he would come right back and ask me again until I finally gave in to his persuasions and said yes. Little did I know that Larry took my "no" at face value and that was that. For several days after he proposed, I thought I was getting married. I started making wedding plans, thinking that any day now he would ask me again to prove his undying devotion. Meanwhile, Cathy was graciously helping me plan every detail of the wedding. An older single herself, she had been through enough of her friends' weddings. She was the classic "always a bridesmaid, never a bride," and had a lot of experience with these things. I, on the other hand, had no idea what I was doing.

"Are you going to have a band?" she said one day. I hadn't even thought about music or a band. *Do you have to have a band to get married?*

"Well, how am I supposed to tell everyone that I danced at your wedding, without a band?" she asked with a knowing smile.

I got a band. The next thing I knew, I also had reservations for a sit-down dinner for almost three hundred wedding guests. Because of the last-minute timing, the only place we could secure for our wedding ceremony and reception was the local country club. I was sure my mother was turning over in her grave. Her only child was getting married with three weeks notice, and it wasn't even in a church!

Cathy came with me to pick out my wedding dress. While we were trying on dresses, I casually mentioned to her that I'd actually said no when Larry asked me to marry him. I thought she'd laugh, but instead she thought I had lost my mind.

"You told him no?" Cathy asked, holding my train as I stood in front of the mirror in my pearl-and-sequin-covered dress. We made quite a pair—Cathy standing in her pale pink bridesmaid's dress and me in my elegant wedding dress, discussing if my wedding was on or off. The woman who had been helping us silently slipped off to the side, shaking her head in disbelief. She thought she'd seen it all until that day.

"Well, are you getting married or not?"

At that point, I wasn't sure! This proposal was not going how I thought it would go at all. Bunching up my train in both hands, Cathy marched me over to the phone at the bridal shop and made me call Larry to make sure this wedding was really going to happen.

I protested all the way, but she said, "You told him no. I'm not buying my bridesmaid's dress until you make absolutely sure you are getting married." The salesclerk dialed the number and handed over the phone with a weak, polite smile. Larry didn't make it easy on me when he answered. He said, "I already asked you. If you want to get married, you have to ask me now." Standing in my wedding dress in the middle of the bridal shop, I proposed to him. Cathy, along with every salesclerk and shopper in the store within earshot of our conversation held their collective breath for his answer. Fortunately, he said yes.

* * *

THE MONDAY after our one-day whirlwind honeymoon to Sea World in San Antonio, in 1991, Larry had to report for duty at Ft. Hood, several hours from San Antonio. For two years, we had a "weekend marriage." Larry came to San Antonio late on Friday and left on Monday morning to go back to work. By the Army's rules, that's called joint domicile. It may not have worked for every newlywed couple, but we actually appreciated the fact that we could ease into living together gradually. After being single for so long, he had his stuff and I had my stuff, and our tastes could not have been more opposite. I'm the essence of clutter, and Larry is the minimalist. He prefers modern with clean lines, and I can't throw anything away!

Because I had no family of my own in America, I bonded with Larry's family, especially his grandfather, Grandpa Ward. Since we'd never had a real honeymoon, Larry surprised me the first year of our marriage with a trip to the Panama Canal with Grandpa Ward and his older sister. They were a pair—he was battling melanoma and she wore a back brace and was a breast cancer survivor. They'd made it this far, so it was no surprise that they survived a river raft excursion down the Martha Ray River in Jamaica, too. Not to mention the fire that broke out on our cruise ship. I felt like taking a Valium every night.

I hate ships, but I loved Grandpa Ward, who became my Svetislava. When I visited him at his assisted living facility in California, I snuggled next to him on his bed and listened to World News on his radio every night until the woman in the next room rapped on the wall for us to turn it down. When he died watching the waves crash on a beach in Santa Barbara from his wheelchair, Larry and I were there. His timely death on the beach seemed like the end of a favorite movie. And another person I loved had now left my life.

After years of intense infertility treatment, my shriveled ovaries gave in and produced our beautiful daughter in March of 1995: Katarina Maksimovich Vukelja Anderson, Maxi for short. Mama was not there when she came into the world, but I made sure Maxi knew all about her *baka* (Serb for "grand-mother"). As a toddler, she would walk down the hallway in our home before bed, touching several of my mother's paintings that I'd purposely hung low enough for her to reach. She'd run her little fingers over them and say good night to the farm animals in the fields Mama painted.

A few months after Maxi was born, the Army began talking about sending us to Bosnia for a year. Maxi was only eight months old, and we would have to leave her behind in someone else's care since the Army would not allow her with us at our post. All I could think about was missing this beautiful baby's first words.

I remember kissing her soft skin one day while singing along to a song, "I Want to Kiss You All Over." At the end of the song, I'd covered every square inch of her little body with kisses—only to finally realize I was wearing red 12-hour lipstick. No matter how I scrubbed, it would not come off! My husband, the dermatologist—and here was our baby, covered in red welts all day! Whenever I thought about the possibility of not being there when she took her first steps, I could hardly breathe. I had served seventeen years in the Army, and Larry had served sixteen—both of us were now Lieutenant Colonels. We decided that was long enough.

About the same time, a headhunter called me with a job offer in East Texas at the Tyler Cancer Center. Tyler was a small town of about 95,000, but it had an excellent reputation in the medical field. After living in major metropolitan cities in America for the past twenty years, it sounded rather small and uninteresting. I wasn't tempted in the least to move there, and if not for this woman's persistence, I probably wouldn't have given it a second thought. She even traveled from Tyler to San Antonio to take us to dinner at one of the nicest restaurants in town. I felt so guilty after all the money she spent on wining and dining us that I decided I at least owed her a look around Tyler. "I should probably just see it, but I'm not moving there," I told Larry that night when we got home. Little did I know I would fall in love the moment I arrived.

During my visit, I met Dr. Gary Kimmel. Soon I knew this was not only the place, but that Gary was the person with whom I wanted to work. I also talked with the rest of the staff about the position and found tears welling up in my eyes. It sounded like the perfect fit for me. I never interviewed anywhere else.

They also arranged for a realtor to show me a house for sale in Tyler. It was in the downtown Azalea District, which had quaint red brick streets and old-fashioned sidewalks. I opened the front door and my eyes feasted on a long hallway with a rich, dark wood floor. I immediately envisioned my mother's paintings hanging in that hallway. I didn't even need to look at the rest of the house. I was sold. Everything about the city and the job and the house felt so right.

A few months after my visit, we were packing our things— but we were not going off to war in Bosnia. Instead, we were leaving the Army and moving to Tyler. I joined Tyler Cancer Center and Larry opened a private dermatology practice.

After almost two decades of service in the Army, I'd forgotten what civilian life was like. Could I leave my known environment and well-rehearsed routines in order to establish a life for our family outside of the Army regimen? I wasn't sure. What I also didn't understand was that even though I was leaving one army, I would soon join the ranks in another one: God's army.

* * *

IN OUR new civilian life, we could volunteer for new challenges and get involved with the community in ways we never could before. Larry's practice was doing very well, and I became deeply involved in breast cancer awareness and education in Tyler and the surrounding area. For the first time since my mother's death, I finally felt as though I was on a clear path. More seeds had fallen onto fertile soil and were taking root. I had a family of my own and more direction and stability in my life.

Nevertheless, I was still searching for something that had escaped me thus far—something spiritual that was hard to define. When Maxi was baptized as a baby, I made sure a Methodist preacher, a Catholic priest and Chaplain Clark, who was a Baptist preacher, were all there "just in case." I'm not one to question how things work up in heaven, so I wanted to make sure she had all her options.

Personally, I was still feeling indebted to the Catholic Church for all they had done to get me to America. I was well aware that without them I would not have had any of these opportunities. Larry and I visited different churches, but in the end I always felt that joining another church was somehow being disloyal to the Catholic Church and disrespectful of all they had done for me.

When another doctor friend, Craig Harrison, asked us to his church for the tenth time, we accepted his invitation only out of courtesy. However, Craig would not leave anything to chance, so he offered to pick us up and take us with him. If you ever want to invite someone to church, that's the way to do it. Don't even give them a chance to make an excuse! I remember covering the phone with one hand and shaking my head "no" while saying to Larry in an upbeat voice, "Craig wants to pick us up and take us to church tomorrow!"

"Find out what kind of church it is," Larry whispered back.

"What kind of church is it, Craig?"

"Baptist," he said.

I freaked out. But what could we say now? We were stuck. The next morning he and his wife, Catherine, picked us up bright and early. After just one visit, we never left. It became home.

Before my mother and I had lived with the Jesuits, I had never been to church, and I had only attended a few times since. This new church was teaching us to read and study the Bible for ourselves, something I had never done; we were also learning to apply this information to our lives.

People whose lives were different from anyone or anything I'd ever known now surrounded us. Something about the people in our church and Sunday school group seemed especially grounded. Their roots sank deep into a purpose for living that I did not have. And suddenly they were all around me. I discovered that my friends, the Harrisons, had given years of their life to serve as missionaries in Africa before moving to Tyler. Around that same time, I also realized many of my staff and patients were concerned with my spirituality, too. Even my nurse, Donna, was a very openly spiritual person. One day, a patient came to tell me he was stopping further treatments for his cancer. Usually, patients just call to tell me that, but he insisted on coming to see me in person. When I walked into the room, he said to me, "I know I'm dying, but I'm worried about my doctor."

I raised my eyebrows, surprised at his candor. "You're

worried about me? You're dying, and you're worried about me? Now, why is that?"

He looked me square in the eye. "I know where I'm going, but I can't leave just yet because I am not sure where my doctor is going."

Where was I going? I couldn't forget his question and his genuine concern for me that day. More and more, I seemed to keep running into people like him who lived with purpose and peace despite the news that they had cancer. Later on it became clear that people like this patient had been beside me all along, but I was just now opening my eyes and seeing them in a new way.

It reminded me of finding wildflowers in the spring that you never knew were there. You didn't plant them, but these unexpected backyard discoveries are beautiful in their own way. All winter, something had been happening underground that you couldn't see until finally the conditions were right for the beauty to break the surface.

I realized this was a picture of the spiritual dimension of my life. All the people and experiences from my past had planted a tiny seed in me along the way. Or God himself had planted it—I still wasn't sure. Whatever the case, the seeds that I thought were scattered rather haphazardly had come together, taken root and flourished underground. And one day, they unexpectedly and mysteriously took on a life of their own and came to the surface where I could see them—really see them—for the first time.

I recalled the Jesuits and the family of nun sisters in the Austrian Alps. I remembered the hours I would lose myself in prayer on the cobblestone floor at the Jesuits' chapel. My mother's prayers to St. Jude. Father Svoljshak's careful handwritten notes on the prayer cards the Jesuit brothers had given me. My first Bible, another gift from the Jesuits. My patients. Chaplain Clark and his daughter. The Harrisons and our friends at the Baptist church in Tyler. And now many of my patients were talking to me about God. *Why is that? Why am I here? What does God want me to do?*

Not only did these events from my past start to make sense, they started to connect in ways that I hadn't thought possible before. Prior to this point, I'd always pictured my life as unrelated memories that happened here and there with no particular significance between them. In my arrogance, I had my own explanation for what things meant and why certain events happened the way they did. However, I could now connect the dots and see they were all coming together in a way that surpassed my superficial explanations. The roots, some decades old by now, were firmly intertwined underground. Everything I'd experienced in my life was actually working together and drawing me closer to a time when it would all make sense. I just didn't know when that day would come, but I knew I was getting closer.

My husband Larry was having his own spiritual reckoning. I remember the day he decided to become a member of the church. In our worship services, we usually sing a song at the end so that anyone who wants to know what it means to be a Christian or a church member can come down the aisle and speak privately with the pastor at that time. We were singing "Come as You Are," as we did every Sunday, when Larry suddenly gathered his Bible from the pew as if he were going to leave. I tugged at his sleeve and said, "It's not over yet. We're singing the last song."

"Yes, I know," he said and continued to make his way out

of the aisle.

"Where are you going?" I whispered, loud enough for the people in the pew behind us to hear.

"I'm going to join the church," he announced.

I was confused, even livid. How could he join the church without us, his family?

He must have caught this from the look on my face because he stopped, leaned back into the pew for a moment and said softly, "This is not a family affair; this is a personal decision." He was right. But I wasn't convinced.

To make matters worse, Maxi wanted to go with Daddy! Embarrassed, I held her little arm and said, "You just stay here with Mommy."

It was actually a few more years after my husband's decision to join the church before everything came together for me, too. It was right after 9/11, the tragedy that brought many people to their knees. Many years earlier, I was in World Trade Center Tower Two when I proudly became an official American citizen. I remember the day I took the oath of citizenship. Mama and I were waiting our turn to take the citizenship test—a test for immigrants to answer general questions about American democracy and/or American history. An Albanian man who had just taken the test walked over to us to whisper some advice. "If they ask you who the first president was, his name is George Washington Bridge," he said proudly.

However, now it was years later and that memory inside the World Trade Center quickly faded into what I was seeing take place on the television. What we all witnessed that horrible September day brought the truth of our own vulnerability to the surface. Even though I was working with life and death every day in my job, this was different. I was familiar with the prelude of death—a prognosis that would often eventually lead to death, but not necessarily right away. On 9/11, thousands of seemingly healthy people were gone in an instant.

That same week, I was scheduled to go to Taiwan to give a lecture on the latest breast cancer treatments. A pharmaceutical company had planned the trip for me over a year ago, but because of the disaster everything seemed uncertain. No one was flying anywhere. People were advising me that it was not a safe time to travel, much less to go halfway around the world with my entire family in tow. To make matters worse, the news was reporting terrible typhoons and floods in that part of the world. I had to decide whether to continue with the trip, and I couldn't ignore the pressing question: *What if something happens to me?*

I kept thinking back to what one of my patients had asked, about where I was going after I died. What was my next step? Was I going anywhere at all? I realized I wasn't sure. I had lived with uncertainty for most of my life, but things had always somehow worked out. However, I had a definite feeling that this wasn't going to work itself out on its own. And this time I didn't have my mother reassuring me or my husband telling me that everything would be fine. I had to make up my mind for myself.

What struck me most was how kind and patient God had been in allowing me to put the pieces together. No matter how I had failed to see him at work in my life in the past, it was never too late. Because of my Catholic background, I had always felt compelled to do a number of good things to earn God's favor, but there was no guarantee that, in the end, it would be enough. What I understood now was that it could never be enough. God loved me no matter what I did or did not do. And it was never too late. God has left the decision up to us—and we can make it at any time. Even if someone has waited so long that the train was now leaving the station, he or she could still get on board and make it to the next stop.

The week after 9/11, I decided to be baptized as an adult and make my decision public. The night before, a friend informed me that I should have made an appointment so the church would expect me. I thought I would just show up like one of the "walk-ins" at our clinic. We never turn them away, and I was certain my church wouldn't either. But when I showed up, I was somehow already on the list.

Entering the warm water of the baptistery, I asked the pastor if I could express how I felt about this moment. I'd seen people being baptized before and most of them answered the questions softly and quietly left the baptistery. When I came up out of the water, I literally felt born again and full of joy. I jumped up and splashed the water, surprising everyone in the pews—and even waking some people up!

I later said I would have jumped higher if not for the wet robe weighing me down. I have never felt such release and an overwhelming sense of peace and happiness. I was in Taiwan with my family the following week, without fear, because now we were all "tucked in." I was not afraid. If something happened, we would all go together to a good place.

We went to Hong Kong, Shanghai, Peking and ended up in Xian where the terra-cotta warriors are on display. In the other cities, our Chinese tour guides were punctual and dressed as if they were going to a wedding. In Xian, a cute, young college-aged girl wearing tiny jeans and white sneakers bounced up to meet us, thirty minutes late. She could have passed for a twelve-year-old. Following her, we piled into a rickety old van with more holes in the seats than cushion. I had to convince my daughter, who was now six, that it was okay not to wear seat belts (which were conspicuously missing from the van) because we were in a foreign country. At the same time, the Chinese driver was methodically chewing on something dark between his teeth, which I later found out was beetle nut—a natural sedative!

To distract Maxi from the chaos, I started to make small talk with our guide, asking about her family, but idle conversation is not really my gift. I inherited another gift from my mother—the gift of asking the unexpected questions. I'm short on small talk. I prefer to get through the layers of superficiality and zero in on things that really matter. So, in the context of all the temples we were passing by, I asked the young guide if she believed in anything. She quickly answered with the party line. "No," she said. Then she turned back to me and added off-handedly, "The government tells us to believe in ourselves." Her voice changed. "But I have a need to believe in something else."

I must have looked shocked at her honesty, because she paused and started to apologize. I told her there was no need to say she was sorry and that I knew exactly what she meant because I'd had the same need to believe in something myself. I realized I suddenly had a new role to fill. I could now influence other people. I was thinking, "I may be out of the Army, but I'm in God's army now. This is my first assignment!"

We spent the rest of the day touring Xian and talking about faith and God and our beliefs. I was new at this, only a week out from my baptism, but I was already starting to recruit!

When I returned from our trip and people asked me about China, I told them about all the tourist sites that, if you have the time and resources, anyone can go and see. But my memories of being at the Great Wall were nothing compared to the connection I felt with this young girl who was searching for something to believe in. I knew I'd planted a seed in her, just as so many had done for me in my lifetime. My "roots" wrapped halfway around the world and, however shallowly and briefly, they had touched hers.

There is nothing more rewarding in life than to connect with other people on a significant level. Fortunately, I work in a field where there are no layers and very little pretense, so it makes it that much easier for us to affect each other. People who are sick and needing help are vulnerable, open and exposed, and I have always found the most ordinary lives become extraordinary in those moments.

As my daughter said to me, when I first began writing about my life, "You can't finish this book because your life is not over yet." And she's right. There are more dots to connect and more seeds to be planted. Life needs to go on. The new seeds need to grow and find their connections with other people. It takes time—it's never immediate. Like wildflowers appearing one spring day, it happens when and where you least expect it. One of the most unexpected seeds that God planted in our lives bloomed in our home one Christmas. His name is Boris.

* * *

"WE HAVE your little boy," the voice on the other end of the line said in a thick Russian accent.

"I'm sorry, I think you have the wrong number." It was the fall of 2004, and I was in Atlanta at a conference, packing up to return to Tyler that night.

"Wait! Don't hang up!" the voice pleaded. The voice on the phone was Natasha, an adoption coordinator for an orphanage in Russia. When she identified herself, I suddenly realized what this puzzling call was about.

In order to explain, I have to go back two years earlier to when my friend Becky had hosted a fund-raiser to raise money for a Russian orphanage. I bid on Becky's prize—a free night of babysitting at her house.

Since I find it impossible to throw anything away, I found the unused babysitting coupon in a drawer two years later. Larry and I were going to a function that night and frantically looking for a babysitter, but we weren't having any luck.

Desperate, I phoned Becky and asked if I could drop my daughter off at her house. "If I don't do it now, Maxi will be in college before I ever get around to using that coupon," I teased. However, I was already in the car on the way over to her house, Maxi in tow.

That's when I came across the Miracle Christmas project. A handful of orphans from the same Russian orphanage were planning to come to Tyler for Christmas to experience life in America for one week. Because she was in charge of organizing it, Becky had photos of orphans and information spread out all over her kitchen counter. She asked me to sign up to be a host home. I thought about Maxi, eight years old and going on thirteen. She had just crafted her three-page Christmas wish list and was reading it to me on the way over to Becky's home. I thought having a little Russian orphan girl around Maxi's age in the house would help all of us appreciate what we already had. I envisioned the girl and Maxi sleeping in the same bedroom like sisters and happily sharing some of Maxi's clothes.

"Sure, put us down for a little girl," I said quickly, kissed

Maxi goodbye and hurried out the door to our event. Never thinking that Becky would actually need me, I didn't even mention it to Larry that night.

Now it was almost Christmas and Natasha, the adoption co-ordinator, was visiting Becky in Tyler to make last-minute ar-rangements for Miracle Christmas. That's when Natasha phoned me in Atlanta. Not only was I needed as a host home, but they wanted me to take a little boy instead of the girl I had imagined. What would Maxi have in common with a little boy?

"This isn't going to work," I told her. "Maybe next time." I started to hang up the phone and so I could finish packing my bags and catch my flight back to Tyler that night.

"This is a special little boy," the woman urged. "We don't have any other family for him." It was a combination of her pleading and my guilt that made me agree to come by Becky's in a few hours on my way home from the Tyler airport.

I pulled up to Becky's and walked to her door. Natasha was standing beside Becky when they opened the door and she gasped, "You look just like your little boy." I recognized her voice immediately. After our phone call, I wasn't so sure that she didn't tell all the prospective hosts something like that to pull at their heartstrings, but when they showed me a video of the boy at the orphanage, all my initial resistance melted. He bore a striking resemblance to me with his mop of blonde hair, angular face and light-colored eyes. His name also happened to be Boris, like my grandfather Boris Maksimovich. On the video, it was plain that Boris was painfully shy at six-and-a-half years old. He did not interact well with large groups, although he clung to a few people. He had sores on his lower lips. When he finally arrived in Tyler in December, the day all the host parents were supposed to meet their children, he wouldn't come near us.

However, by that evening at our home, he was snuggling up with Maxi, who nurtured him as if she'd been a big sister all her life. And he was working his way into our hearts as well, calling Larry "Papa" and me "Mama"—the only English words he knew. It was gut-wrenching to think this was only a week out of his life before he would have to return to Russia.

At the end of the week, the entire family was convinced he was meant to stay with us—me, Larry, Maxi (whom Boris had taken to calling Maxia in his Russian accent) and even the dog. We could not send him back without promising him we would come get him later that year. As a reminder of our promise, Maxi gave Boris one of her favorite stuffed animals: Simba from *The Lion King*.

On his last evening with us, I told him in Russian that when he opened his eyes the next morning he would have to go back home. Not surprisingly, he stayed up until after midnight, forcing his weary eyelids, swollen from crying, to stay open. Boris held Simba tightly under his arm and boarded the bus the next morning bound for the Dallas airport. Deep sadness washed over all of us like a wave of physical pain. At one point, Boris looked over at us standing there waving to him and let out a mournful cry that sounded like a wounded animal, as if the pain of leaving was squeezing his very soul. A stream of teardrops fell from Boris's cheeks onto Simba's fur, drenching the stuffed toy that he clutched to his chest.

Six months later, all three of us flew to Russia to begin the proceedings and finalized the adoption on a second trip. The first morning after we brought Boris (and Simba) home, I went in his room to wake him up and he opened his eyes, smiled and said, "I was hoping you would be the first thing I would see."

Maxi took to Boris and her role as a big sister as if she'd waited her whole life for this to happen. However, after Boris had been with us a few weeks it began to dawn on her that things were very different. Two children now shared the attention—not only ours, but everyone's at school and church. So many friends wanted to know about the newest member of our family. One day she burst into tears and said in a child-like but perceptive way, "I feel like an old dog and Boris is the new puppy. Everyone wants to play with him and know his name. They're always asking me, *Where'd you get him? What is his name? How much did you pay for him?* And then there's me—the old dog that no one's interested in anymore." I was speechless. For a moment, I panicked that I was bringing such joy into one child's life while destroying the other one at the same time. However, Maxi had been part of this adoption throughout the entire process and just needed reassurance.

I took her in my arms, looked at her and said, "Maxi, this puppy is not going back to the kennel. He's here to stay. Besides, every new puppy grows into an old dog someday. And there is more than enough love in this house for both of you." She looked at me, smiled softly and said, "Okay." And that was the end of that. Boris and Maxi are growing up to be more and more like their father—generous and giving. I remember Maxi's first Halloween I dressed her in a Dalmatian costume and took her with me to the hospital while I did a consult. On a whim, I stuck lollipops all around her car seat to give out to the patients and nurses. Ever since then, both our children have done a "reverse Halloween" at the hospital—instead of getting candy and treats, they give them away to patients and staff.

The longer I'm a mom, the more certain I am that I was born at age thirty. I have no idea what it's like to be a kid, as my daughter (who is now a teenager) reminds me every day. Some people thought I was out of my mind. Here I was, 52 years old, adopting a seven-year-old boy who spoke not a word of English. But that didn't scare me. When Maxi grew up and wanted to wear makeup at age thirteen, it sent a small shiver up my spine. But still, that didn't frighten me. What really scared me was the threat of cancer coming to my own doorstep, and I suddenly realized how much I had and how much I could lose.

CHAPTER TWELVE

HOPE RINGS ETERNAL

I t started with an abnormal mammogram. Many of my patients' stories start much the same way. A cheery nurse in pink scrubs squeezes the patient's breast into a machine until it feels as though half of the chest wall is going with it. Then the doctor's office calls back, but they don't explain exactly why. Another phone call to come back for another test. Another ultrasound. Then it dawns on the patient: something's very wrong.

When they called me back after my routine mammogram, they said they wanted to re-check it. Their offices are in my building, so I took the elevator up there three different times that same morning. Turns out, I had abnormal calcifications that were new since my previous mammogram. I would have to wait and have some other studies done before I could talk to the radiologist to discuss the findings. Not in my wildest dreams did I think I was going to have something abnormal, but for the next week, not knowing the significance of this discovery was horrible.

Everything just seemed to stop at home while my family and I talked about the next steps. In the first 48 hours, I realized something right away: my family could not function without me. Everyone was acting as if I were already dead, and we didn't even have a diagnosis yet!

The doctors wanted to "watch" this abnormality over time

to see if anything came of it, but I knew I did not have the patience to watch it. If something was in there that did not belong, I felt it needed to come out—and my surgeon, Dr. Andrews, agreed. I had a lumpectomy to remove the calcification, and in the process they also discovered an incidental benign tumor. I was lucky.

I have always known from the time I was a young girl that nothing in life remains the same. Not your home, not your relationships, not your plans. Not even your body. My breast cancer patients often tell me how their breasts are never the same after surgery. They sometimes ache with the changing weather, and the regrowth of nerve endings can produce the oddest sensations. To me, it's all just a small reminder of the larger truth that change is part of being alive.

Receiving a diagnosis of cancer is one of the biggest changes a person will ever face. Cancer patients often ask me, "Is it terminal?" I always say the same thing—terminal is a bus station. "This is the wrong clinic if you want to live forever," I tell them. Life is terminal. If you are alive, you will one day die. My job is to keep it from happening prematurely.

Usually, patients also want to know what their "chances" are, as if a percentage or statistic can indicate that. I tell my patients they don't have to be a statistic. Everyone is an individual case. I understand patients wanting to know how long they have to live, but I never give a number (though I may tell them that their time can be measured in months). One of the reasons I don't assign a specific number is that none of us knows how long we have to live. One of my patients was diagnosed with cancer, but her husband died unexpectedly months before she did. She went to her chemotherapy on the day of his funeral because she said he "would not have wanted me to miss my treatment." Dr. Jerry Nielsen, who discovered she had breast cancer while serving at a base at the South Pole, once addressed a breast cancer conference in Tyler. "It doesn't matter how or when you die," she said. "The only thing that matters is *did you ever live? Did you?*" After meeting her, I know she *lives.*

Live, live! Don't just exist. Many of my patients have a sense of the limited amount of time remaining on the clock, and they want to live it all. I will never forget a ninety-three-year-old patient who would not wait twenty minutes in the lobby for her appointment. "Twenty minutes is all you had to wait?" I asked her, knowing I am always running late. "If you've only been waiting twenty minutes, this is a good day! Where are you going?"

She informed me that if she only had a limited amount of time left on this earth, she could think of better ways to spend it than waiting in a doctor's office! I enjoy connecting with patients on that level. I love it when I encounter someone who has stripped off the layers of superficiality we so often wear.

I sometimes wonder if some cancer patients aren't born with an intuition about the brevity of their life. Many of them live such robust, full lives prior to their diagnosis that it's almost as if they somehow knew this was going to happen to them one day. My patients live so much in such a short period of time right until the end. Very few of them just exist between their visits to the clinic. They consume every minute of life—there is nothing wasted.

This was how Peaches lived, and how she died. She was my patient in the clinic, but my friend outside of the examining room. Even though her name was Peaches, many people who knew her well put bright yellow lemons in the flower sprays at her funeral. She'd often said that when life hands you lemons, you make lemonade. She had so much spontaneity. Sometimes she would just show up at my office with a wild story to tell me or something she just wanted to show me. One time, she appeared at my door dressed in a red shirt, green pants and purple shoes—as if she couldn't limit her outfit to just one color. Her personality was as colorful as her clothes and her paintings.

She was not afraid of dying. Her faith was so strong. Toward the end, she was tired and did not want to undergo any more treatments. As her doctor, I was frustrated because I was certain there was so much more I could do. However, as her friend, I knew she wanted to go home—her eternal home. One day, toward the end of her life, she reached out with her soft hands, brought my head to her chest and said, "Thank you for loving me." I never stopped loving her. She lived well and finished well.

* * *

IN THE PROCESS of writing this book, I realized it's no coincidence that I have given my life to work with cancer patients. Those who respond well to treatment share a common identity with those who escape the ravages of war: they are survivors. I closely identify with survivors because I am one. I know what it's like to slog your way through whatever life throws at you for no reason other than you must. Everything inside of you is pushing you to go forward, because there is no turning back.

I remember a woman at a Race for the Cure event: a fundraiser walk/run for cancer research that many breast cancer survivors attend. She was filling out her registration as big tears rolled down her cheeks, splashing onto the paper. I asked her why she was crying.

"I just don't know what to put here." She pointed to the form.

"What do you mean? Just put your name and address."

"No," she said, weeping. "Here, where it says to check this box if you're a 'survivor.' I don't know if I am one or not. It hasn't been five years yet."

I stood beside this woman, who had obviously recently been treated for cancer, and said, "Are you talking to me right now?"

She said yes.

"It's really you and not some double or something?"

A weak smile escaped her lips and she wiped her nose.

"If you are talking to me and you have been diagnosed with cancer, then you're a survivor."

Survivors are not just survivors of a disease. You could survive a bad marriage. You could survive rebellious children. You could survive a car wreck, the death of a child or a house fire. Any number of things can make you a survivor if you do one thing: refuse to give up.

I prefer survivorship to "cure" because *survivor* covers a broad range of things. Cure is a four-letter word to me. It has no meaning. Plenty of people in cemeteries today were "cured" from cancer but eventually died of other things. There are also people who are cured but miserable. They are constantly worried the cancer will come back and they don't give themselves permission to enjoy life. Healing, on the other hand, is vastly different; this is why healing people and keeping them in remission is my focus. *Healing* is about getting to the other side of a malignancy. We are all potential patients. Some of us have just not yet been diagnosed.

In the Bible, there's a story in the book of Luke about Jesus and his disciples in a storm on the Sea of Galilee. Despite the winds and the heavy rain, they were able to get safely to the other side of the lake. I tell my patients, "No matter how bad it gets, I'm going to get you to the other side. It may not be a smooth journey—and there will be times when the boat may feel like it's going to capsize under the size of the waves. But, one way or the other, you will reach the other side."

I'm convinced we will eliminate all cancers, and we'll do it through research. My belief explains why I feel the need to keep my patients alive long enough for the right drug to be discovered. I believe we will one day talk about the demise of cancer the way that we talk about the plague or small pox. We need to get rid of it. And we will.

Cancer, like the adversities my mother and I went through, can teach you how to die, or it can show you how to live. Kris Carr, author of *Crazy Sexy Cancer* and a cancer survivor, said that cancer was not killing her—it was "forcing me to live." It can make you better or it can make you bitter. After all, cancer is just another seed. Once it takes root in your life, it will either overtake you like an ugly weed or, with the right treatment, will bear fruit that brings a changed perspective and a new purpose for living. In fact, I've seen the unexpected beauty that blossoms and blooms from someone's cancer experience continue to affect everyone around them, sometimes even long after they are gone.

I remember when Deborah, the wife of a local physician and a cancer survivor, came for her first treatment. She was holding a glass vase of exotic cut flowers that I assumed was a gift for me or my staff. I told her, "Deborah, you should concentrate on yourself and your treatment today." She laughed and said, "These are not for you." Curious, I wanted to know why she brought flowers.

"They're for me," she said with a brave smile on her face, her eyes sparkling. "I want to be surrounded by beautiful things today."

During her treatment, she stayed in a private room we have in the back of the clinic, usually reserved for people who are too sick to be in the main area or those who need more privacy. When she walked in, I thought I saw a flash of dismay in her face. Her disappointment did not come across as a complaint—she seemed to be merely sizing up the room's potential in her mind. I don't mind complaints—if someone comes up with a solution to fix the problem. Reading her thoughts, I told her she was welcome to make any changes to the room she wished.

Soon, she transformed it into her vision of what a healing room should look like. Under her direction, it became a soothing environment filled with comfortable furniture, softly lit lamps, a prominent cross on the wall and some artwork she had painted.

I gave her a journal and repeated what someone had once told me: "If you're living it, it's worth recording." Deborah not only journaled, she captured her cancer experience through her paintings and writing, ultimately publishing a book called *Journey: Painting and Poetry*. One of my favorite poems she wrote is "The Vein":

As the blood flows through the vein
So does the medicine with great pain
While avid preparations are made
Our memories fade, and fade
Into different shades

SEEDS

So colorful and intense
The body waits in suspense
-*Deborah Stephen, ©2002*

Her attitude, so full of life, generosity and giving, is what helped her survive. We have since painted together many hours, connecting art and beauty and sharing it with others by displaying it in the clinic. Deborah proves that what someone makes out of cancer is what matters. As a friend of mine once said of this disease, "There is no recovery, only discovery." Cancer can be a wake-up call. I tell patients that life will never be the same, but it could be better. And for many, it *is* better.

A woman once told me cancer had taught her how to live and made her realize who she was deep inside. She wouldn't trade the experience for anything in the world. Cancer doesn't take anything away; it's the something extra. If you let it, it works in your favor and helps you see life and yourself differently so you can focus on what's important.

When I was young, my mother and I could close the door and leave everything we owned behind, but we always carried our identity with us in Mama's plastic bag full of documents, photos and certificates. We never let go of the unchanging inner core of what made us who we were.

People who are diagnosed with cancer struggle with this. They are so caught up agonizing over the disease that it robs them of who they are. They become the cancer, when just the opposite is true. They are still the person they were before the diagnosis. They may be an engineer. A school secretary. A mother of four. Now they are all that, plus they have cancer. They have not lost anything. They actually have more.

My best patients are the ones who go on to live their lives

and forget that they even had cancer at one time. Not losing our sense of who we are is very important to me. But it doesn't have to be. It's not part of my job. I could simply focus on my patients' disease and not on anything else. However, I'm convinced that when people remain focused on the person they are inside, they're better equipped to fight and better prepared to survive.

When I see someone letting go of a key element of who they are, I intervene immediately. One of my patients was a talented artist, but I did not know it. She was diagnosed with breast cancer, had a mastectomy and stopped painting. When I took her history, I asked about her hobbies. She said to me, "I was an artist, but then I got breast cancer." I had just read an interesting article about a series of paintings that an artist had created using live elephants' tails as brushes. He dipped their tails into various paints, then splashed them onto the canvas and called it "art." I told her about the article.

"Did you paint with your breast?" I deadpanned.

She was speechless, not certain she'd heard me correctly.

"I can just see it," I said, cupping my own breast in both hands and "dipping" it into an imaginary can of paint. "You dip the nipple in the paint and make the dots. That must be an unusual technique."

She offered a quiet "No," clearly mystified by my demonstration. Undaunted, I did some further investigation. "Oh, I know, maybe the surgery damaged the nerves in your arm, so now you can't use your arm to hold the paintbrush. That must be why you don't paint anymore."

"No, there wasn't any damage," she began.

I pretended to flip through her chart. "Well, I don't get it then. Why can't you paint?"

She got it. I know she got it because she began to see herself as an artist again—but not just an artist. An artist with breast cancer. One who underwent a transforming experience that has brought blessing and perspective to her work. *Not recovery. Only discovery.*

I asked her to bring me some of her work and made room on the walls of the Chemo Gallery we created at the treatment room in the Tyler Cancer Center. When I first hung several pieces of my mother's artwork there, someone commented that the room now seemed more like an art gallery than a chemo room.

With Peaches' help, I promptly changed the name to Chemo Gallery. Art reminds my patients that they are bigger than their cancer. I prefer to think of going through treatment as "getting past the bump in the road of life." That's all it is.

In fact, my daughter Maxi, a talented artist herself, created a series of paintings to hang in the children's wing of a local hospice. Boris did one too. We framed the huge paintings of elephants, monkeys and giraffes for the children to enjoy. Patients can look at art and be swept away to another time and place. The Chemo Gallery at my clinic helps patients get through the bump in the road in a nourishing, pleasant environment, filled with soothing music, colorful fish, paintings and an abundance of smiles and hugs.

I wrote this book in part to give my patients a better understanding of myself and why I do what I do. But I've been tempted, as we all are, to lose sight of who I am along the way. For example, I wore the same thing to work every day in the Army: black flats and my uniform. When I got out of the Army and rejoined civilian life, I was introduced to wardrobe possibilities I never had when I was in the service. But that brought problems, too. I worried constantly about sitting properly in a skirt, having a glaring run in my pantyhose or that my earrings did not match my outfit. After a while, I decided I had to get down to the basics again. Just me. Scrubs and clogs. I had to come just as I was, or I wasn't coming at all.

The only wardrobe exception I allow myself these days is to wear the outrageous socks patients have given me over the years. (I tell them my socks must cost five dollars or less or I get a rash.) It's always a refreshing icebreaker in the midst of a serious conversation about death and dying if a family member looks down and notices the sparkly, checkered or polka-dotted socks on their doctor.

* * *

I TELL my patients when they receive a diagnosis that they have to move their name to the top of the page, which is hard to do. Most of them are so used to taking care of everyone else that it's unnatural to let others take care of them. For years, their needs have come after their children's needs, after their spouse's needs, after work and the house and even after the family dog. Sometimes they're not even on the list at all.

When we're well, everything and everyone is ahead of us. You can't do that when you're a patient. When you're sick, all the energy needs to go to you for a transient period of time. That's the only way to resume the role of taking care of everything and everyone else. Those receiving treatment need to receive care instead of being a caregiver. I've found that people need permission to let go and let others care for them. Likewise, family and friends who want to do something to take care of their loved one need a green light to do so.

My mother and I could not have gotten where we did without the generous help of others. At times, we were wholly dependent on them, unable to get over the next hill unless they helped us. With rare exceptions, everyone I can recall—the Jesuits, the Regouts—all the people along our journey were helpful. Like the Southerners I met when I first came to Texas, most of them were nice to us for no good reason. I have to believe that God was orchestrating all of it, bringing these people into our lives at just the right moment. What a tragedy it would have been if we had refused their assistance, thinking we had to make it on our own somehow. Cancer is something that affects the entire family, even if only one person is diagnosed. No one can fight it alone. People often have a fear of leaning on someone else because they don't want to become a burden. If Mama and I had ever given in to those same feelings, we would not have made it.

I also tell my patients that part of their therapy is to pray. There is no insurance coding for prayer or prescription for prayer treatment. It's cheap. You can do it anytime. And there are no ill side effects—no nausea, no vomiting and no hair loss. Best of all, it works. One woman I treated for breast cancer began praying immediately before she even started treatment and the tumor began to shrink.

I used to be very streamlined in my approach to cancer treatment. My philosophy was to identify the "bad guys" and then go after them and keep fighting. I had a rational explanation for everything. I once knew a patient when I was in DC that was basically sent home to die. It was around Thanksgiving and they had to send him home in an ambulance because he was so weak. However, he kept insisting that he could not die because he had to see the birth of his grandson.

I asked him as he was leaving, "When is your grand-son due?" That's when he told me that his daughter wasn't pregnant. In fact, she wasn't even dating anyone at the time. I thought he was off the wall for having such an ambitious outlook. One day, years later, I changed my mind when we had a visitor at the front desk. An older burly man with a Grizzly Adams beard and flannel shirt was standing there, holding the hand of a little boy beside him. I had no idea who he was until he spoke.

It was the patient sent home to die years earlier. His de-termination to see his grandson arrive was so strong that he lived to see it happen. At the time I wanted to have a logical explanation, since there are examples when lymphoma sud-denly spontaneously goes into remission. But something else told me it was a medical miracle.

Today, I want to use everything we have at our disposal to fight cancer, and I believe prayer is often helpful, though it may be the least-used weapon in our arsenal. When we're sick, we feel out of control. We can't give ourselves the treat-ment we need. However, prayer puts some measure of control back in our court. For many of my patients, prayer was already a significant part of their lives long before they received their diagnosis. We simply encourage them to continue praying, in addition to receiving the radiation, chemotherapy or surgery we provide.

I used to pray in a global sense, uttering something like "God, let us all be happy" as I pulled out of my driveway on my way to work. And my prayers were usually just a reac-tion—*after* a catastrophe had already happened.

I still pray in the car going to work each day, but my prayers have changed over time from being knee-jerk responses when something bad happens to something I do every day *to prepare me* for that day.

Prayer has also evolved into something more personal. When I lived with the Jesuits, I prayed for hours on my knees, reciting rosaries and other mantras. Mass, especially when conducted in Latin, was an effective way to focus my mind and keep my thoughts from drifting. Yet I never experienced the sincere, conversational prayer I now realize I can share with God. I had to learn to pray this way. It happened subtly, but I learned from my patients that prayer is something you have to do expectantly, with no doubt in your heart. There's no wishful thinking—only the certainty that things are going to happen.

I captured this positive outlook in a bronze statue I had commissioned for our clinic. It's a life-size sculpture of a breast cancer patient and mother of three. Ironically, she was a drug rep for the chemotherapy agent that was used to treat her. Her steadfast commitment to her own survival mesmerized me. I said one day when she visited me, "That look on your face right now—that's what my patients need to see." I asked her if we could sculpt her expression—a triumphant and bald survivor, radiant with hope. Her bronze image now greets every visitor who enters the building.

When you merely wish something would happen, you leave room for ambivalence. Many of my patients are so sure of the power of God and his will that they *know* it's going to happen. And you know what? A lot of times it does. God answers my prayers, but I have to say that I'm always still surprised when he does.

One of my patients was diagnosed with stage 4, non-curable cancer. She was a simple woman, and I assumed her happy disposition was because she did not grasp the severity of her disease. One day, I came right out and asked her, "Why are you so happy?"

She smiled and said, "I'm blessed. I get up in the morning and if I'm alive I say, 'Praise the Lord!' When God wants me, he can have me. But in the meantime, I'm blessed." If her positive expectations "failed" and she died, she would never even know it! In fact, she lived much longer with her disease, despite all statistics. She was truly blessed, and I was blessed to know her.

* * *

I AM PAYING attention to different things these days. I have long discussions with my patients about the fact that none of us are going to live forever. And I talk about that right up front. There is no time for sugarcoating reality. I don't have all the answers—but I'm not afraid of raising the questions so we can talk about the inevitable at the front end of the disease, when they're still coherent enough to discuss it. At the end, it's too late. I tell each patient what I know about their case, and then we deal with the unknowns.

Many times when a patient is sitting in my office and hears that he or she has cancer, the news is met with great tears. My response is to try to dissect their emotions and understand why they are crying. Most people tell me they are not afraid of death itself. It's dying they are afraid of. They are afraid of whatever they believe dying means. They don't want to suffer or put undue stress on the loved ones having to care for them.

There's a poem by Linda Ellis called "The Dash," which talks about being at the funeral of a friend and the importance of living the little "dash" between your date of birth and date of death that will one day be engraved on your tombstone. I tell my patients that our purpose in undergoing treatment is to stretch that little dash. If we're successful, they have more room to stuff more experiences and love and laughter into "the dash."

I've discovered there are three kinds of cancer patients. First are those who get the diagnosis and go into denial. At first, they believe it can't truly be their test results—it must have been a mix-up. Then they want second and third opinions. I often never see these patients again because they're off trying some unconventional drug or therapy in Canada or Mexico. Then there is a second kind of patient. They hear the diagnosis and immediately stop living. Their family members weep for them and huddle close together with their arms around each other. The family answers my questions for the patient, as if they're no longer in the room. Then there is the third kind of patient, who is empowered to take control of their diagnosis and treatment. They are on your team from the beginning, carefully taking notes and asking many questions. One question in particular always comes out at the end of our conversations: "When can we get started?" Together as a team, doctor and patient, we can accomplish a lot with and for this kind of patient.

I actually find that second category the most rewarding— picking up the patients who are down, even though it is work and takes a lot of energy from me. I've always been able to cheer people. Like my mother did for me, I want to keep them afloat so that they don't focus on their circumstances, but on surviving the next thing.

Mama always told me it was going to work out, and I believed her. Part of the reason is because you're more likely to believe someone who has *been there* and tells you it's possible to get through it. A breast cancer survivor and friend of mine named Freda is that person for the hundreds of survivors she helps educate every year. She believes women should love their bodies more than their doctors do, and be an active member of their healing team. She encourages women to do everything in their power to equip themselves in the fight against cancer. She poured out her passion for survivors by helping me organize the first Race for the Cure event in Tyler and starting a support group. I often turn to her with newly-diagnosed patients who need help taking charge of their care and their life. Freda is my patient, but she has also been my right hand. She's almost become like a member of the family.

So many of my patients have inspired me with their courage and determination. It would be impossible to tell each of their stories here, though I am tempted to do so! They may not be part of this book, but they will always be part of my life.

In fact, my patients and I often draw strength from each other. Tina was one of those special patients. She is an angel that I know I can see. Even when she was at her sickest times, she often wrote me notes to encourage me and tell me she was praying for me. She saw rainbows everywhere and interpreted them as signs of God's presence. One day, there was a little feather on the floor in her hospital room. She carefully gathered it into a plastic baggie to show me later.

"Look!" she said when I came in. "The angels were here earlier."

She was a very well-educated advertising and marketing executive and had developed a speaking ministry for cancer survivors. After she had extensive treatment for metastatic breast cancer, which she'd battled for over twelve years, she underwent surgery to remove part of her tongue because she had developed tongue cancer.

After her mouth surgery, I was concerned about how it would affect her level of speech. To tell the truth, I couldn't help but wonder what more could possibly happen to her. When I entered her room the day after her surgery, I tentatively said, "Tina, how is it?"

Tina opened her mouth and sang with a warbled voice, "Ahh-le-lu-lah!" I couldn't believe my ears.

"Satan thought he'd be able to keep me quiet, huh?" she said in a garbled voice, and laughed aloud. Nothing could keep her childlike, boisterous spirit quiet.

After all that she went through, she developed brain lesions and was struggling with the decision to undergo radiation. "It's my *brain*," she would say fearfully, still waiting on a sign from God—something to tell her what she should do.

One day I stopped by my office on the way to see Tina while she was up at the Cancer Center discussing her options with the radiation oncologist. I grabbed a free scarf one of the drug companies had provided for cancer patients and carried it under my arm as a gift for her, since her hair had recently fallen out. As I was leaving, a magnet fell off my filing cabinet. I picked it up and was surprised to see it was a rainbow magnet. I tucked it into my pocket to show Tina, knowing she would get a kick out of it.

I showed her the magnet and gave her the scarf, which she promptly unfolded. We were both shocked at what we saw. I'd never even unfolded the packet it came in, but the scarf Tina held in her hands was rainbow-patterned. As if that weren't enough, in the course of our conversation Tina looked over my shoulder and saw two more rainbows. One was a puzzle of Noah's ark with a rainbow arched above it: someone had framed it and hung it on the wall inside the exam room. The other rainbow appeared on the front cover of a travel magazine lying on the table.

"That's God!" she shouted with glee. "I know I'm supposed to do the radiation now. I just needed a sign to make sure."

She came through radiation and lived longer than expected, but not nearly as long as I'd hoped. After she died, I recalled that each time after she was hospitalized, she would announce, "Think of all the new people I've reached." Her obituary accurately listed her occupation as advertising executive and evangelist.

The childlike spirit she had touched us all. To Tina, the beauty of God never became blasé. On her birthday, only a few months before she died, she took me by the arm and, with her face beaming, told me, "This is my year." And so it was.

When one of my patients dies, it takes a lot out of me. I am tempted to be hard on myself, wondering what else I could have done. But then, on the same day, it often happens that another patient will finish her last radiation treatment or another will have a clear CAT scan. The smallest triumph will inspire me to keep going. Sometimes I've questioned whether it's good for me to be so close to my patients. After Peaches died, I went to see a friend and patient of mine with ovarian cancer. "I can't do this anymore," I told her. "I can't get close to you guys." Cecilia stopped me with a simple question.

"Are you better off knowing me as a friend, in addition to being your patient?"

I knew in an instant my answer. And so did she. Anticipating my response, she said, "And I'm so much better off knowing you," and grasped my hand in hers.

I will never forget helping Cecilia be there for her daughter Sophie's first day of school. She was so afraid she wouldn't live to see that special day because she was so sick. Knowing how much this meant to her, I arranged to sneak her out of the hospital that morning. I pushed her in a wheelchair myself from her room into the parking lot and into my car, as my heart raced. I was silently praying that we'd make it to school and back without a major incident! Her skin and lips were ghostly pale, but Cecilia's face glowed when she saw her daughter's desk and met her teacher before we scurried back to the hospital, unnoticed. That evening she rested easy, her wish fulfilled.

It was Cecilia's idea for the mosaic around the celebration bell at Rose Rudman park in Tyler. Cancer survivors can ring this bell, inside a white gazebo, and send a beautiful note of hope resounding throughout the park. Patients contributed every piece of the mosaic inside the gazebo. A bottle cap with a peach on it from Peaches. A piece of blue pottery from Cecilia's favorite coffee cup and a sliver of glass on which she had carefully written the word, "faith."

We have a celebration bell at the clinic, too, and we aren't shy about ringing it. We ring the bell when someone completes the last round of chemotherapy. We give it a hearty shake when we're celebrating a good test result. Sometimes, I'm in one exam room delivering the news to someone that they have breast cancer and the bell will ring, creating a sense of hope that only a moment before was nowhere near.

"Why a bell?" I once asked Cecilia when we were discussing her plans for the gazebo in the park.

"Because hope rings eternal," she told me.

I agree. The loneliest place in the world is not sickness.

The loneliest existence is to be sick and have no faith, no family and no hope. I've heard my pastor say that H.O.P.E. stands for Having Only Positive Expectations. In a specialty like mine, there are many unknowns. For the most part, people have a problem with change and the unknown. We prefer to deal with black and white issues that we can easily define. Cancer doesn't work like that. And, as I learned early on in my journey, neither does life.

I learned to live with the unknown because of something my mother believed: when so much is unknown, there is no reason *not* to have hope. Hope was a seed my mother held in her hand so that even when the sun's rays grew dim, the nurturing warmth of human touch would take their place. For years, we never knew what would happen next to us. Change was the norm, not the exception. But somehow, it always worked out. My story is one of hope and the courage to embrace—not just endure—change. When you least expect it, even the smallest, oldest seed of hope can surprise you.

I was reminded of this when I read about scientists who discovered seeds inside a clay jar that were over 2,000 years old. They carefully planted them and waited to see what would happen. Weeks passed. Nothing. They watered. Nothing. Fertilized. Still nothing. No signs of life, day after day, for six weeks. Just when the whole experiment seemed like a waste of effort, a tiny green sprout curling on top of the soil appeared— just like the new growth of curls dotting the proud heads of my cancer survivors. Irresistibly soft patches of peach fuzz give way to these unexpected strands of hope after life's longest, darkest season. However, the color and texture of the new hair always come as a surprise. Their hair, like everything else, is rarely as it was before. It too has changed.

SEEDS

It takes courage to endure change in our lives, because of the pain that often comes with the process. In biology, in order to release what's inside, a seed's shell must split wide open and break. Sometimes life does that to us, too—splitting us wide open at our most vulnerable points—and it's painful. But it's often at the point of pain when the transformation begins and the seed begins to grow.

If we are too frightened of the future and too scared of the unknown to risk change, we'll just remain a seed in the darkness underground, never knowing what might have been in the light of day. When we refuse to change, we begin to die. But the moment we are willing to change is the moment we really begin to live.

Live. Live! Don't just exist.

* * *